PRINTHOUSE BOOKS
PRESENTS

I0024220

TAHIRY
True Fiction

ANTWAN 'ANT' BANK$

Tahiry

©ANTWAN 'ANT' BANK$; 2014

PrintHouse Books, Atlanta, GA.

Published 8- 3 -2014

www.PrintHouseBooks.com

VIP INK Publishing Group; Incorporated

ANTWAN BANK$

Cover art, designed by SK7.

ISBN: 978-0-9911719-7-2

Library of Congress Cataloging-in-Publication Data

ANTWAN 'ANT' BANK$

Tahiry

1. Drama   2.Erotic   3.Crime   4.Urban Literature

5. ANTWAN 'ANT' BANK$

Tahiry

In the City of Atlanta; the Gentlemen's Club Industry reign Supreme. Alongside the fledging music industry that contributes platinum hits every other month, together they both pull in Billions of dollars each year. You would actually have to live here or frequent the ATL to see the marriage these two have committed to each other.

The biggest misconception is for someone to assume that it's all illegal. What many don't know, is that the city of Atlanta benefits off of every Stripper, Bouncer, Waitress, Dj and Bartender that works in the Gentlemen Club Industry. The truth of the matter is, for any girl wanting to Strip here in the ATL clubs, such as Onyx, Majic, Strokers, Pin Ups, Shooter, Follies, Blue Fame, Blaze, Oasis, Cheetah, Pleasers, Diamonds, Babes to name a few, and trust me there many more! You must first have a permit, from the County that club is in, before you can even think about dancing on any stage in this city.

Yep that's right! These permits can only be obtained from the County Sheriff Department where they perform a thorough background check for Felonies and any open Warrants. If you have a conflicting felony you will not get a permit! If you have a warrant, you will not be leaving through the front door but going to the back in handcuffs instead. Permits range from $250-$475 per year depending on which club you are getting a permit for (That's every-year!). How do I know, you ask! Well, let's just say when I first got to the A, I took a Doorman position at one of the most notorious clubs in Atlanta where I met thousands of dancers whom led me to write this story. The club shall remain anonymous because they fired my butt for hustling too hard; Hell I was just trying to show them how to get paper. After all, I did just close a club back in South Khak that I ran for 12 years.

Anyway   that's   another   story.

Regardless of what you may have seen or heard, the competition in these clubs are fierce and that makes for some slow nights when it come to the cash flow for some girls. So some of them, more times than none; take it to the next level and do what they like to call private parties. For you squares out there, that means Escorting, or Tricking if you want to keep   it   street.

I found myself in an interesting position while working at this ATL Gentlemen's club. The dancers confided in me and asked me to be their driver to some of these so called private parties. The stories from those nights and from other private discussions we had while riding in my car, was unreal! My true passion and God given talent is a writer, so I had to ask these girls if I could tell some of their stories; while keeping them anonymous of course. I was happy as a

Kid in a candy store when they agreed. So here it is; several accounts of the ATL night life through the eyes of many dancers that I rolled into one character, whom I named Tahiry. Laced with Cocaine, Molly, Weed, Lean and Z-Bars, this life is in no way, full of glitz and glamour, true crime rides along at every turn, from the streets of ATL this is our story, cold Hearted and Street Official. R.I.P to the dancers we lost to the Strip Hustle. We got love for you.

Tahiry

Dedicated to the ladies trapped in the hustle, living with the stigma of the Strip game. I got love for you, only you know your struggle and what measures you need to take to survive.

ANTWAN BANK$

ANTWAN 'ANT' BANK$

Tahiry

True Fiction

**VIP INK Publishing Group,
Incorporated**

Atlanta, GA

Tahiry

Table of contents

1. East Side

It's 2011 on a warm July day; Tahiry's neighbors blast Rocko's new hit; "Dis Morning" while outside grilling some chicken and ribs not far from her bathroom window. Tah sings along with the track as the beat vibrates through the Valley Ridge Apartment complex, over in Decatur while actively listening from the shower through her open window. Warm water drizzle down her light skin, flawless body, as she lathers, Dove soap all over. Tahiry slowly massages the sponge over her healthy C cup breast then down her flat stomach all while rapping with the music.

"This Morning, I woke up" "Feeling like Money" "I jumped up!" "Put on my Gucci's and my hat." Then a loud male voice from the bedroom suddenly overshadows the music.

Damn baby; play with that pussy for me, come on and show it to me! Meshaw you're going to get in trouble; what if Tahiry see us? Come on baby, she's in the shower; so hurry up and show me that wet-wet!

Okay hold on; let me fix my web cam. Yeah that's my girl; let me see that thang! Meshaw sits up in the bed then adjust his laptop atop of the pillow so he could get a good look at her while she focused the camera on her vagina for him to see. He slides off his boxers, sits up in the bed and massages his penis while she fingers herself on camera for him.

Yeah you like that Meshaw; this what you wanted? Yeah finger that cock girl, damn it looks good. Ummm; it feels good too baby. When are you coming over to fuck me for real? I want you inside me. Shit; I'm coming tonight baby, as soon as I get rid of Tahiry's ass! Meshaw! Meshaw! Oh shit; she's coming! Meshaw, who are you talking to? Nobody baby! Yeah right; you lying motherfucker; whose on that laptop, I know I heard you talking to somebody; I aint crazy. Nobody Tah!

Tahiry, naked and dripping wet; snatches the laptop off the pillow. What the fuck; why are you naked, where's your drawers nigga! Oh hell nah; who is this bitch! Oh; you having web cam sex with this ho! No Tah! Wait a minute! Fuck you Meshaw! Bling!

Tahiry slangs the laptop through the bedroom window. Girl; why in the hell you do that shit! Damn, that thing cost 800 dollars Tah! Yeah that's right, go get it, you better get your trifling ass out of here! I can't believe you Meshaw; you got all of this right here and you got the nerve to be jacking off to a bitch on the computer! Girl, aint nobody been jacking off shawty; we were just talking.

Miss me with that lame ass excuse Meesh! Whatever Tah; you better hope my computer aint broken or your ass is going to buy me a new one. You better tell that cyber slut to buy you another one. Smack! Smack! Who do you think you're talking to like that Tahiry; you better watch your mouth! Tah falls back against the bedroom wall from the two heavy blows Meesh delivered to her right cheek. Sweat combined with water, now drench her gorgeous body as she watch Meshaw walk out of the front door to retrieve his laptop.

Frantic, she moves herself away from the wall, grabs the car keys off the coffee table then runs outside naked. Kids dribbling their basketball; stopped then let it roll down the parking lot as they stood in awe of Tahiry's, wet, naked body; running across the apartment lawn to her black Ram Charger.

Meesh walks over by their bedroom window to pick up his computer that was shattered into several pieces. Vroom! Vroom! Vroom! He jumps up, alarmed at the sight of the charger then starts screaming as the grill came charging at him. Oh shit! Tah! Tah! Stop! What the fuck! Thump! Thump! The Charger accelerates in drive then reverse, then back in drive again as it pins Meesh legs against the wall under the bedroom window. The neighbors stand around looking at what had become a tragic turn of events as the music still bump, weed still burn and cell phones took pictures of what was surely going to be the talk of the hood for the next few days.

Tahiry leans out of the window, shouting. Yeah you sorry ass motherfucker, I bet you won't hit me again, huh nigga! Vroom! Vroom! She reverses the Charger then drives it forward once more then left it in park, pinning Meshaw at the knees while stuck against the wall as Dekalb County Police Sirens; get louder and louder by the second.

With the engine still running, car in park, driver's side door open and wooden patio fence shattered, Meshaw in pain and sit stuck between the wall and the front car bumper. Police officers arrive to a hectic scene as Tah sits on the trunk of the car naked like everything was normal. Excuse me Ma'am; what happened here? That faggot slapped me in my face then walked outside like it was ok; so I came out behind him, started my car then ran his ass over. Now can I press charges on his ass?

Yes Ma'am but can you come inside and put some clothes on first please? Why; everybody out here has seen a naked woman before. Ma'am you can come in willingly or I can escort you down to my house, we have a nice cozy cell for you and some blue scrubs too.

Hell, we'll even feed you, if you're hungry. No, that's ok officer I'm going. What about him; are you guys going to take that woman beater to jail? Yes we are; now can we get you some clothes.

Tahiry jumps down from the trunk and walks back inside the apartment to retrieve some clothes while the officer wait outside the door as neighbors stand there enjoying the show.

Man why yall taking me to Dekalb County shawty; she the one that ran me over. Calm down Meshaw; she pressed charges against you. For what, I aint do nothing! She said you hit her man. Come on shawty; I aint hit that girl, she lying!

Well, my partner says that you are on probation anyway and this right here just violated you my man. Damn shawty; it aint even got to be like this bruh. I'm afraid so Meshaw, now put your hands on the hood. For real shawty, I can't even walk and you gone hand cuff a nigga. Yes sir, after I get these cuffs on you, my partner will help you walk over to the squad car. Oh yall gone help me walk huh; aint this a bitch!

Two royal blue couches, a flat screen, 52 inch T.V and glass end tables sit in the front room of Tahiry's small apartment. In the same room but divided by a counter and book shelf sits a small kitchen with a laundry room off to the right. As Tah exits the bedroom of her apartment now fully dressed, she steps into the bathroom then puts on some deodorant. Knock-Knock! Yes come in! Are you dressed Ma'am? Yes officer!

Ok great, I just need you to complete this police report so we can be on our way. Sure whatever you need sir. Well, why don't you tell me exactly what happened before we got here. No problem, I was in the shower when I heard some voices coming from my bedroom. At first I thought it was the T.V but Meshaw's voice caught my attention. It sounded to me like he was in my room conversing with another bitch. That's when I finished up my shower, stepped out of the tub, butt ass naked, still wet and made my way to the bedroom.

What happened next, Ma'am? That sorry ass punk was in my bed, jacking off to some stinking bitch that he was chatting with on the computer. I ran over to the bed, snatched the laptop then tossed it through the bedroom window. We argued about that for a minute and that's when he smacked me. I was shocked because he had never hit me before. He went outside to get his computer and I ran out after him, only to get revenge. As soon as he bent over to pick up the pieces to his laptop. I jumped in my Charger and ran his punk ass over, as many times as I could until you guys came. I want yall to put his no good behind, under the Dekalb County jail for hitting me. Don't worry Ma'am we will do just that. Thank you! You're welcome Ma'am. You can call me Tahiry officer, I'm no Ma'am!

Ok Tahiry; thanks for your cooperation, we will be taking your boyfriend down to the station now to book him. He will have a hearing sometime tomorrow if you want to be there. Child please; that nigga can kiss my ass. I don't play that domestic violence shit; he's lucky I aint kill him. Yeah; I'm glad you didn't go that route Tahiry; no one has to die here. Do you see how big Meshaw is officer; look at me! I'm 110 pounds and that fool 6'3"

260 pounds; I can't fight that man! Like I said, he's lucky I didn't kill him. Yeah I guess he is; well if you need us for anything else, don't hesitate to call. We're headed back to the precinct. Thanks again officer! You're welcome and have a good day Ma'am.

Over on East Ponce De Leon Ave.; the scene is kind of mellow as Swayzee and Skeeta shoot a game of pool during dayshift at Pin Ups. The purple lined tables and bright colored carpet showed all its flaws this time of day with only a few patrons inside. While the music bumps, A dozen naked women straddle men at the back bar while giving $5 lap dances during the dayshift.

Hey Swayzee; what yall having baby? Let me get 20 of those jerk wings with that Raspberry sauce and a few Corona's Tia. Ok be back in a few baby. Thanks shawty.

Come on and break Skeeta; I know you scared of this ass whipping, I'm about to put on you. Whatever Sway; you aint won a game yet partner; what makes you think I'm gone let your monkey ass win this one fool. Break shawty and stop talking all that shit. Ring-Ring! Ring-Ring! Get your phone Sway; you got time to talk, I aint leaving your ass no shot anyway. Ring-Ring! Boy you're talking a gang of shit, aint you! Ring-Ring!

Hello, who this? Yo Swayzee; what up my nigga, this Meesh. What's up shawty; where your ass at; I heard they took you to County? Hell yeah shawty; them fools about to break me off with a nickel on this probation violation. Damn my nigga; sorry to hear that shit. It's all good Sway; I might as well go ahead and get this time done so I won't be on no paper when I get out. I hear that folk; what you need me to do on the streets for yah shawty.

Just look after Tah for me bruh; she aint got no paper coming in and all my work is out on them streets; you feel me? I feel you; who owe you? That boy Truck on the South Side and Nook over on the West End. They aint gone give you no trouble though; they good peeps. Alright shawty; I'll bag that for you and I'll make sure Tah is straight too. Good looking out my nigga; I have to get off this phone, be safe on them streets and keep trill my nigga. No doubt shawty be easy.

Damn Skeet can a nigga get a shot? Yeah on the next game; I'm about to put this 5 ball in that side pocket then put that 8 over in the right corner. Man your ass just showing off in front of these strippers. Aint nobody showing off Sway, you just mad partner; who was that on the phone? Oh that was Meshaw; that fool got a nickel shawty. Damn, what he want? Want us to get some money off the street for him and asked me to look after Tahiry too. That fool, ask your dog ass to look after Tah for him; he must be tripping.

Skeet, I'm gone beat that bad ass pussy up on a regular; you feel me. I'm gone be like 2 chainz; hair weave killer up in her pretty red ass. Yo; Tahiry high maintenance bruh. So what; I got paper Skeeta; that's my bitch now nigga. Yeah whatever; rack em, so I can beat your ass again. Here's your wings Swayzee and two Corona's. Thanks Tia! Come on and let's eat Skeet; later for that game shawty. Alright, I'm coming, damn those wings smell good!

Yo; look at that sexy red bitch over there Skeeta; I'm cutting that today; my dick hard just looking at her ass. Which one Sway? Right there with the white boots on Skeet, wearing the two pony tail braids. Oh yeah that hoe is fine; her girl bad too. I'm about to call them over and see what's up with the private party. Go ahead do that shit Skeet; I'm down.

He waves the two dancers over to their table. They gather their drinks off the bar then walk over to the guys. The girl on the left; stood 6'1" in her white boots with six inch heels. Two long black pony tail braids hung down the center of her back as she seem to glide over towards them. Her bow legs resemble a stallion as she walked, holding her thongs in her left hand and drink in the other. The fluorescent lights glisten off her smooth red skin, flat stomach, perky breast and Cartier eye glasses. Her friend stood a little shorter in her pink; knee high; stiletto boots which complemented her chocolate skin, tone abs and firm butt. What's up fellas, yall want a dance?

No shawty we're trying to see what's up with the private party; what time yall shift end? We get off at 8; how much money are you trying to spend baby? How much do you charge red bone; don't be hitting a nigga in the head neither shawty. For you; I can do $250. I know I get an hour for that and some head too right? What's your name before we start doing business? Oh my bad baby; I'm Swayzee and that's my nigga Skeeta. How you doing Swayzee; I'm Flawless and that's my bitch; Stallion.

Ok now that we're all acquainted; what's the business after work? We'll I told you my price; your boy has to talk to Stallion about her prices. Shit; he cool over there, so you guys driving or do we need to pick yall up. Nah we cool; I got a 650 and she has a Range. Damn; stripping paying the bills huh? Yep; you aint know? Shit; I do now Flawless with your fine ass; say, are you gone let me eat that pussy too? I don't know; you got to be gentle with my kitty. Do you even know how to eat pussy; if not I can get my girl Stallion over there to show you how it's done later.

Nah I don't need no help; I can handle mine. You kind of cute Swayzee; I like tall, dark skin men; how come you out here tricking; you aint got no girl? Yeah but this here is fun, you know; some extra-curricular activities and shit. Oh is that what you call it? Yep! Well; where are we meeting you guys after work? We can meet over at my place in Decatur. Where is that Swayzee? Off of Covington and South Hairston. Oh ok; I don't stay far from there; I'm off Redan.

Cool, so let me get your number Flawless and we will call you two around 8 or something like that; I hope yall burn because I likes to smoke before I cut; you feel me. Yeah we burn but we will probably be on half a bean by the time we get there. Ok that's what's up shawty; we'll see yall later then. Ok Swayzee; here's my number; that's a nice hair cut you have too. Thanks Flawless.

So; I hope you like fat boys. I don't discriminate honey; how come they call you Skeeta and you a big boy? Skeeta sounds like somebody skinny. It's a long story; how much are you gone charge a nigga? $250 for you teddy bear! Oh; I'm your Teddy bear huh? Yep; can I call you that; my sexy Teddy bear; you kind of remind me of - Don't even say it! Why not? I already know what you are

33

going to say! Then it's true; you heard it before, Ruben! Yeah, yeah whatever; I don't look like Ruben Studdard. I think you do and that's a good thing. Hey Skeeta; let's go shawty; we have some business to take care of. Girls we will see yall later. Ok fellas; see you around 8, right! Yep! Swayzee and Skeeta, finish off their drinks then head for the exit as the two dancers watch them leave.

Knock-Knock! Yeah who is it? It's Kodi bitch, open the door! It's open girl! Oh hey, what's up; how you doing? I'm good, just watching T.V; what you up to? About to walk over to Publix, come go with me. Bitch it's hot as hell out there, I aint walking nowhere. Girl; bring your pretty ass on, you aint doing shit but watching Lifetime. What you going to get Ko?

A few steaks and some potatoes! Damn who you cooking for; you must got a nigga coming over; I see you got a new hair style too. Girl stop it; my ass just high and got the munchies. We can cook it over here if you want. You can cook it; I aint good with steaks Kodi; your shit will be messed up. Ha-ha! Tah you a fool; put your shoes on and come with me. Alright girl, hold on a minute.

I heard about Meshaw; when is he getting out? I don't know and don't care; I am done with that fool. When did you get your hair done; it looks good. Thanks Tah! I'm going for a new look;

Tahiry

I'm getting a new tatt tomorrow. You just have to mark up that mocha skin of yours; don't you girl? I keep telling you that you're too pretty for all that non sense. I know you aint talking Tahiry; you got about four tattoos yourself. Yeah but- Save it bitch and let's go!

Kodi; Tahiry's friend and neighbor stood 5'7" with a slim build, fake D cups, fake bootie and smooth mocha skin, a dime piece in any man's book. Alright, I'm ready, let's go; I can't believe you got me walking to Publix. Girl it's only across the street, your ass aint gone die. Maybe not but it sure as hell feel like it. So how are things, are you still at the Stroke House? Hell no, aint no money in that motherfucker right now Tah. I think I'm gone try Follies and Shooter Ally for a while; I heard they was poppin.

Damn don't you have to get another permit to work at those clubs? Nah both of them are in Dekalb County, I can use the same permit I used at Strokers. Oh that's cool right there! Yep; I can use it at Pin Ups, Blaze and Oasis too. Damn all of them? Um-hmm! Beep-Beep! "Hey shawty; come here and let me holler at you!" Ha-ha! You heard him Kodi; he tryna holler at you. Shit, not driving no damn Honda Civic he aint. Girl I got standards! Bitch you fool!

Beep-Beep! "What's up shawty; come here!" Kodi slangs her honey blonde weave to the side then grabs Tah by the hand and runs across South Hairston Blvd into the Publix parking lot. Damn that fool still tryna holler. He'll be alright; let's go get these steaks; a ho is starving!

Ring-Ring! Ring-Ring! Kodi are you gone answer that? She looks down at the phone to see who is calling. Nah he can wait; that's one of my regular clients. Oh excuse me; you got clients now ho? Ha-ha! Yep or you can call him a trick; which-ever; it's all the same. Kodi you're too much. Enough about me, how are you eating? What you mean? I mean, since Meshaw is gone be locked down for 5 years; how is your ass gonna survive out here on these streets?

Shit; I don't know; I guess imma have to find me a new nigga to take care of me. Girl; miss me with that; you're smarter than that, you can make your own doe. How; I damn sure aint shaking my ass in no club; I can't fucking dance no way!

Ring-Ring! Ring-Ring! Damn; can a bitch enjoy some time off. These fools won't give my phone a break. What's wrong; is that your client again? Yeah but this is another one; he's this old guy that comes to see me. Damn; you don't discriminate huh? All money is green honey, doesn't matter who gives it to me. I hear that! Oh yes; this feels good! The cold air hits Tahiry's face as she enters the sliding doors at Publix, Kodi following close behind.

Well Tah, what are you gonna do? I don't know; get a job I guess. Girl please; your high maintenance ass aint gone work on nobodies job. Ring-Ring! Ring-Ring! Kodi; your iphone is blowing up! I know girl, they can't get enough of these D cups and fat ass I got. Ha-Ha! That was the best money you ever spent huh? You damn right; these motherfuckers done paid for themselves 20 times over. Ring-Ring! Ring-Ring! Let's walk back here to the meat isle and get some T-Bones.

Hey Tah; hold on let me see if I brought my cash with me before we try to buy anything. Kodi pulls her red coach bag from her shoulder, looks inside then pulls out her cash. Ok cool! Damn bitch; you get all that from dancing? Kinda! What you mean; kinda? Umm; these look good; how many steaks you want Tah? Fuck them steaks; answer me Kodi? What girl? What you mean kinda?

Well, I don't exactly dance anymore. What do you mean? You just said that your clients or tricks were calling your phone. Yes that's true; come on let's get some potatoes. I'm still waiting on your answer Kodi. Girl I know, we can walk and talk at the same time; come on.

That's a lot of cash you got there Ko! I know and it's all mine, now calm down and I will tell you how you can get some too.

I aint trying to get locked up Kodi! Just chill Tah and listen. Ok I'm all ears. Have you ever heard of Back page? No, what is that? Remember Craigs list? Yep! Well it's just like that but you have to pay to advertise on it. Ok and what does advertising on an ad site have to do with all that money in your coach bag? Ha-Ha! Just wait; you'll see. Don't play with me Ko! Alright, alright; back page has this section where escorts post their ads for dates. Soooo are you an escort then? Yes I am.

The last time I checked that was illegal Kodi! It is but so many bitches are doing it; it's hard for the cops to catch all of us; and Tah! What! This thing is global, I mean there's bitches in every city in the world using this back page thing; it's like the new hustle for ho's! Girl your ass is going to jail for that; I don't want any parts of it. Tah this beats working in clubs by a long shot, aint no tip out, no permits and you make your own hours and set your own prices. You can fuck three dudes in a day and make $1500, $1000, $1200 what-ever you want.

Then once you made enough for the day, you can go party, shop, eat dinner or just watch Lifetime if that's what you want to do. I don't know Kodi, it sounds tempting but I'm not trying to get locked up and have my face all over the news and shit. Not to mention having my picture on a back page so my folks can see it. Girl, you don't have to put your face on it. You can crop your face out or use a body double. Ho's do it all the time.

Hello ladies; did you find everything ok? Yes ma'am, I just have these two steaks and the potatoes. You should think about it Tah; I can show you the ropes. Your total is 38.93 Ma'am. Kodi pulls two twenty dollar bills from her knot then places it back in her coach bag. You ladies have a good evening and come back to see us. Sure and you do the same! Tahiry responds then gets back to the conversation. So how you do it without getting caught?

See, they have these Vanilla pre-paid Visa cards you can use to pay for the ad. This way no one can trace who published the ad on back page. The other thing you will need is a burner phone or one of those pre-paids that no one can trace to you; never use your real number; that's how bitches get caught up. The money comes so fast and easy; that ho's forget that this hustle is illegal. And if you don't remember anything else; remember to always listen to your gut! It will never guide you wrong; the minute you go against your gut feeling is when your ass get busted.

I'm still kind of hesitant Kodi; that's a lot of dicks to be fucking every week. Aren't you scared of diseases and shit? Girl that's why you always use condoms; for sex and oral, always, always! Me, I don't let those nasty tricks eat my pussy or kiss on me, Lord knows what kind of germs they got and where that mouth has been. You set the rules and tell your clients what's allowed. The object of the whole game is to find a few good clients that you can depend on, on a weekly to monthly basis then live off that money they pay you.

Girl, I'm gone need a lot of KY jelly! Yes you will bitch and drinks lots of water too. When you look at it Tah; it's really no different than having a nigga that takes care of you. It's just that these men are tricks and all they want is pussy, no strings attached. Now I'm not gone lie, sometimes a hoe can get caught up, especially if a trick looks good and he's fucking you proper too. That's when you have to learn to separate feelings from the business. Don't get caught up, I know hoe's that fall for it every day.

Damn Kodi; what if he's fine as hell though. It doesn't matter; you have to remember he's tricking for a reason. Maybe he has a woman or wife and kids at home and you are just the jump off with no strings attached. Well, I guess you got a point there. So what you think, you wanna try it? I guess I can, as long as you are there with me. Cool, we can do a two girl special tonight; this way I can walk you through your first night. TONIGHT! Yeah, trust me Tah; after the first date you will be straight. I sure hope so Ko!

You will girl, now open this damn door so I can make these steaks. A bitch is starving! Ha-ha! Girl you stupid!

Damn Skeeta, we need to hit a lick real quick shawty. I know Sway but it's still early man; all our spots don't start jumping until night time. Let's see; it's 6:30 right now Skeet; where can we catch some fools slipping? Hold on; let me think bruh. Yo; we can hit up one of those ATM's! Yeah but which one though? Shit; one where somebody is getting money out.

I know that fool; I mean where to? Hey get on 285 and let's go to Lavista. They got those four banks all across from each other. Oh yeah over by North lake huh? Yep! Good thinking Skeeta! Swayzee speeds up the white Range Rover then turns onto 285 North off of East Ponce. Hey; shawty was fine though; wasn't she man? Who, that Flawless chic you was talking to? Yeah man. Oh; she was straight but you know I like my girls chocolate. Now that Stallion is the truth; I'm gone pop me a blue pill and give her ass the business. Skeeta, nigga you 24 years old; why the hell are you popping Viagra?

Swayzee you need to get on it bruh; that pill have you fucking all day, night then again in the morning bruh. Shit my stamina strong like that boy; I don't need no damn blue pill; your ass shouldn't need it either. Keep taking that shit and you gone bust your heart open or something.

Ha-ha! Man shut your crazy ass up; I aint gone bust my heart. All I know is; whenever I take one like an hour before I get me some pussy. My dick doesn't even go down; not even after three nuts. Them hoe's be loving it too; I remember I fucked this fine ass ho from Texas that was here working that back page. That bitch called me for the next two days to come lay this pipe and she didn't even charge me to hit either.

So you saying she was sprung Skeet? Sway I made that freak bust like 8 times; hoe damn near started crying. Man stop lying; you gone make me pop one of them pills if it make you put it down like that. Just let me know bruh; I just got my new order in the mail today; two new packs, 24 pills. Damn; your ass is serious huh? What; nigga be hitting the pussy like superman Sway! Ha-Ha. You crazy shawty!

Wait until you try it; you'll see. Yeah, but do the girls know that you be on the blue pill? Hell no and I aint telling them either. You dirty Skeet! Man I just love pussy, especially that wet-wet; lord that cut up be good bruh. Shit; I feel you on that shawty; I'm gone pop me one tonight when we meet those two pin up hoe's. Alright I'm warning you now, that hoe gone be hooked. She will be calling you every day to come hit that thang. We gone see Skeet; you better not be lying either shawty. Man; trust me; you'll see. Ok bet, now get your burner ready, we gone hit this fool right here at the WFB drive up teller; I'm gone pull up behind them; you get out right here and walk to the front of the car. Ok slow down so I can get out.

Swayzee slows up at the curb off Lavista and the Mall Commons to let Skeeta out of the Range then makes a left into the WFB parking lot located in the Mall Commons. Skeet pulls his Braves cap down over his eyes; pulls his nine from his pants then approaches the front of the Red Mustang as it pause in front of the ATM. Swayzee came to a slow roll behind the mustang until his front end touch the cars bumper just as Skeet approach the driver's window.

Alright; you know what this is; don't fucking scream and nobody will get hurt bitch. "Okay, okay, what do you want?" Give me that ATM card! "Here you can have it!" What's your pin number? I said; what's your pin number; fat bitch? "It's 9876!" Ok turn the car off and give me your keys! DO IT NOW! "Here you go Sir; please don't hurt me!" Shut up; I want $2000.00; you got that much in your account? "Umm" Answer me hoe!

"No; there's only $1400 in it!" Sway leans out of the window and shouts. Nigga hurry your ass up! Hold on; just keep that damn truck running! Alright bitch; there better be $1400 in here too or your ass is gone get shot tonight! "Please don't shoot me sir!" Bitch shut your ass up! Skeet inserts the card into the ATM machine as two cars enter the parking lot while enters the pin. Shawty we running out of time; hurry the fuck up! Man one second; let me get this money. He enters $1400 then waits for the money to dispense. Hell yeah; see, that wasn't so hard was it hoe? "Please can I go?"

Yeah after you find your keys! Skeeta tosses her keys across the street then reaches in the car and grabs her purse. "You can have it sir; please don't hurt me!" He takes out her wallet then retrieves her Driver's License. Now you better not call the cops either or we will come merc your ass. DO YOU HEAR ME! "Yes Sir" Good! He reads the Driver's License then looks at her. It was nice meeting you; Crystal Harrison! Come on fool! Swayzee backs up then pulls the Range off to the side of the mustang, Skeeta jumps in then they peel out of the lot and back onto Lavista. How much did you get shawty? $1400!

Cool; $500 for them hoe's and we can go get us some Pappadeaux's too. You got that bitch license right? Hell yeah bruh; now let's get back to Covington Hwy, so we can change these plates. Man that hoe aint gone call the cops, she too scared! Fuck that Skeeta; I aint taking no chances!

Bitch I can't believe you burned the steaks! Shut up Tah, I'm high; let's just get to the restaurant so we can eat! Ha-ha! Your ass, don't need to smoke Ko! Yeah whatever! Ok we're here! Tahiry pulls into Arizona's parking lot, just over by the Stone Crest Mall in Lithonia GA. The temperature is soaring above 95 degrees as she exits her air conditioned Charger to enter the restaurant. Tah's; thin Red sun dress ripples as the humid warm air blows across the lot while Kodi remain in the passenger seat; back and bottom arched up as she removes her panties from under her see through, ankle long, white linen dress. Tah stops to fix her sandal then notices that Ko isn't walking behind her. Bitch will you come on; it's hot out here! Go in girl and reserve our table; I'm coming! I just have to take these thongs off; I want my pussy to breath. It's too damn hot for panties today! Girl you stupid; ok I'll be inside. Alright be there in a sec!

Ring-Ring! Ring-Ring! Hey Mr. Q; how you doing today; you ready to see me huh; sugar daddy? Yep; what time are you going to be free Kodi? Maybe in the next hour and a half; me and my girlfriend are about to eat some lunch. Ok I'll call you back around then. Alright sweetie; I'm working over by Stone Crest today. Did you want me to come to you, or are you coming to see me? Oh and my girl is working with me tonight also; you can get the two girl special. Really; is she as pretty as you are? Hell yes; I'll send you a pic. Sure; do that! Alright; I'm about to go inside the restaurant; I'll send it as soon as we hang up. Ok; I'll be waiting honey!

Kodi scrolls through her mobile photo gallery, finds a pic of Tahiry, sends it to Mr. Q then walks inside Arizona's. Afternoon Ma'am, did you want to get a table for one? No Sir; my girlfriend should be here waiting on me. Oh the young lady in the Red dress? Yes that's her. Follow me please; I will show you to your seat. Thank you sir!

And here's your table Ma'am; this is Monique, she will be your server. Hi ladies! Hello Monique! So what can I get you guys to drink? Hmmm, let me see; Tah you want some wine? Sure! Ok Monique; let us have a bottle of your Moscato. Ok great; I'll be right back. Hold on baby; bring me some of that Apple Pecan Cobbler too. Damn Kodi; aint you gone eat some dinner first. No; I'll eat that after my desert; don't judge me! Well excuse me! Did you want one too Ma'am? No Monique I'll order my desert after dinner; thanks. Ok I'll be back soon.

Tah this is my favorite place to eat; have you been here before? Yeah a while back, me and Meshaw came to this Jazz night they had last year, chilled outside and had a few drinks. Oh I bet that was nice. It was cool. The food really looks good on this menu though Kodi; what are you getting? I'm getting what I always get girl; the Hickory Grilled; Atlantic Salmon. That is delicious honey; what are you ordering? I think I'm gone try this Hickory Grilled Chicken and Shrimp pasta. Yeah you'll like that; it's really good.

Don't tell me you tried that too. Yep I sure did. How often do you come here Ko? Maybe three times a month; one of my clients likes to eat out before we go fuck. He wants the GFE; that's Girl Friend Experience; if you didn't know. And as long as he is paying; I'll give him the GFE too! Look at you over there Ko; your ass like being a ho; don't you bitch? Tahiry all it is; is sex and time for money. The professional word for it; is an Escort. Ring-Ring! Ring-Ring! Oh, hold on Tah; this is one of my older clients; Mr. Q! Ring-Ring! Hello baby!

Hey I really like your friend; she's cute. How much are you going to charge me to see both of you tonight? Did you want in call or outcall sweetie? Uh; I can

61

come to you all. Well in that case; we can do it for $350 a-piece for 45 minutes. Ok I can do that; what time can I come? Well; we're about to eat dinner now; I'll call you when we're finish. Great, don't forget hun! I won't baby.

You just made your first $350 for only 45 minutes and it's not even gone take his old ass that long. What are you talking about Kodi? That was one of my regulars; I told him earlier that we were doing a two girl special tonight. He wanted to know how you looked, so I sent him one of your pics. He liked it and now he wants to see us after dinner. Bitch you sent my pic to a stranger? Calm your nerves Miss High

Maintenance; I cropped out your face. Oh; ok.

Alright ladies; here's your bottle of Moscato and your Pecan Cobbler pie. Thanks Monique! Your welcome; are you guys ready to order? Yeah; you can take hers first, I'm about to take a bite of this cobbler. Sure, what are you having Ma'am? Give me your Hickory Grilled Chicken and Shrimp Pasta. Alright and are you ready to order now Ma'am? Ummm, this Pie is so damn good! Umm! Yes honey; give me your Hickory Grilled Atlantic Salmon. Ok I have the Chicken and Shrimp pasta and the Atlantic Salmon. Will there be anything else ladies?

Tahiry

Yes; can I have one of those Pecan Cobblers? Yes Ma'am! See um-hmm; I told you! It looks good; don't it? Hell yeah! That's because it is. Tah picks up her fork then reaches over to Kodi's plate for a piece of cobbler. Bap! Uh-Uh; get your own, keep your paws off! No you didn't! Hmm!

You guys are too funny; I'll be back shortly with your cobbler. Don't look at me like that Tahiry Nelson. This is mine; yours coming. See; you aint right! Ha-ha. I love you Tah. Tahiry drops her fork, looks at Ko, smirks then shakes her head.

2. Cash Out

Ring-Ring! Yeah who is it? Hey Tahiry; what's up? Who is this? It's Swayzee! Oh hey Sway; I haven't heard from you in a minute; what you doing calling me? Meshaw aint here; he got a nickel? Yeah I know; that's why I'm calling, he asked me to look out for you while he's gone. I don't know why! I'm not his lady anymore; that punk put his hands on me! Well, I hear you on that but my folks asked me to look out for you and I'm gone do, just that. Whatever beef you and him got is between yall shawty.

Umm-hmm, whatever Swayzee! Well I need to get my hair and nails done; are you gonna help me with that? If that's what you need, I got you. Yeah you want some of this pussy; that's all that is Sway. Since you brought it up; Kodi told me that you were in the trap with her last night. What trap boy; you know I aint slinging no dope. Nah, I'm talking about that kitty; I heard about your back page gig. See I'm gone fuck Kodi's ass up!

Calm down Tah; it's all good shawty, that's why I wanted to speak with you. What; you got $500 to spend on this sweet pussy? Hold on Tah, hold on! For what; I need cash; a bitch got bills nigga! See, I got a way for all of us to get a check. All of who Sway? Me, you, Kodi and Skeeta! Man you gone have my ass locked up with Meesh, fucking with you; I don't know about that Sway. Just hear me out Tah and if you don't like the idea then I won't bring it back up. Alright I guess so. Cool; I'm about to put on my shoes; meet me outside by the mailboxes and we can go get some lunch over at Pappadeux's. Boy; your ass still eating at that place? Damn, I know you go there at least four times a week!

That's my spot Tah; we can go somewhere else if you want. I'm cool; we can still go there. Ok meet me outside in 10 minutes. Damn Swayzee; that lil nigga gave us some Mid! I knew we shouldn't have trust that Nawlins fool. Skeeta; shut up and just smoke that shit. Oh I'm about to; I paid for it, I'm smoking it. I wouldn't care if it was Reggie! Yeah I already know; I'll be back in a few. Where you going? I'm taking Tahiry to lunch so we can chop it up about that business. Cool; I'm gone sit here, smoke this blunt, eat this cold ass chicken and watch some of this SVU marathon. Alright shawty, save me some of that smoke too!

Nigga get your ass out of here; I aint saving you nothing. Skeeta stop tripping! Man, take your tall, dark skin Stoudemaire looking ass on; I was just playing. Fuck you Skeeta! Skeet takes a toke off the blunt with his right hand, grabs a cold church's drumstick with the other, lean back on the couch then turns up the volume on the 52" flat screen that's taking up the entire right wall of their small living room.

Ring-Ring! Hey Kodi; what's up? What you doing Skeet; smoking? Yep, you know it; what's the business? I got an outcall over in Marietta; can you take me? What time you need to be over there? I told him 3 O'clock. Yeah I got you; it's gone be $75 though. Don't even play me like that Skeeta; you know I always take care of you. Well I was just letting you know because I aint got time to be driving way the hell over there and that trick back out on your ass.

He's one of my regulars; so you don't have to worry about that. Ok cool; walk your ass over here then; I aint driving to the back of the projects to get you. Shit; I'm paying your fat ass; I don't see why not! No Kodi; you're paying me to drive to Marietta not around the damn corner. Ok I'm coming but I need to shave my pussy before I go. Handle your business; I'll be right here at the house. Alright see you in a minute Skeet. Yep.

It's about time Tahiry; it took your ass long enough. Don't start with me Swayzee; what do you have to talk with me about? Get in and close the door woman, it's hot out there; you're letting the AC out of the Range. Tah; jumps up on to the butter soft leather; Range

Rover seat. Damn it smells good in here nigga; you just cleaned it? Baby I keeps the Range clean; this white don't take long to get dirty. I hear that big timer! Anyway; what's going on? Like I said on the phone; your boy wanted me to look after you. I already told you Sway; I aint with that fool no more. Ok but hear me out; I've been thinking and the two of us should go into business together. Nigga I don't need no pimp, because I'm on back page don't mean I'm stupid. Damn shawty, slow your roll; it aint even about that.

Then what is it about, Sway? Let's go to Papadeux's and get something to eat and we can talk about it. We don't have to go all the way on Jimmy Carter to talk at Papa's; we're talking now. Besides; I have to post later so I can make me some money. Alright we can ride and talk, is that cool? Yeah that's straight; turn on some music too; what you got in here? It's some cd's in the door panel over by you; put something in. Ok cool. Tahiry looks through the cd's as Swayzee pulls out onto Covington highway, makes a left then down to South Hairston. What the hell is this? What you talking about Tah? This Dirty Sprite Cd! I don't know; I just got it from the Texaco up the street; off the Mix tape rack.

Hmm, it says Future; Dirty Sprite; let's see what this nigga is talking about. Put it in then Tah and let's see. Hold on

Swayzee, can a bitch get the cd out first; damn player. We're gone take a ride over to Fulton Industrial; I need to pick up something anyway. Really Sway; way over on the damn South Side! Yep, it won't take long; I'm going straight up I-20. "It's all about little Mexico!" What the fuck? I don't know what that was Sway; hold on let me try this one, right here; "Watch this with Rock." "Lil Mexico Nigga you see it!" "FreeBandz Nigga!" "Aye watch me watch every dance" "Watch me light up them list" "Watch this chain how it shine." "Watch wink and I kiss." Yeah I fuck with this right here nigga. Oh you like that Tah? Hell yeah; what you don't?

Nah it's ok; it aint that hot to me. That's because your ass over there hatin; just drive this Rover and I'll Dj. Let me see what else is on this Dirty Sprite joint. Ok; I see he got one with Tity Boi too. Aint that shawty from that Duffle Bag Boy cut. Who you asking Swayzee; I don't know. Yeah I think it is, play that joint; let me see what's poppin. "Yeah Yeah.. Yeah, Yeah Yeah.. Yeah, Yeah Yeah.. Yeah" Now that's A one right there shawty, hot ass chorus. Shut up Sway so we can hear the lyrics. Turn it up then! Tahiry turns up the volume as they take the I-20 West exit off of Wesley Chapel rd.

"All-white bitch to match my all-white Louies." "Millionaire frames hand-made; I'm just coolin." God Damn; was that that Future nigga Tah? Yep! Yeah; let it ride shawty just play the whole shit. Oh; now you like it! Girl let the damn cd play and stop talking shit. Man you niggas a trip; always be hatin on somebody until you see a bitch like me on it. Tahiry gone with that bullshit and put on your damn seat belt! I'm about to put you up on this street business. Let me just say that I'm not selling no kind of drugs Sway! No Molly, no weed, no ex, no coke, no bars, none of that!

Me neither Tah; that aint my thing! Alright then what is? See me and Skeeta take what we want. We like search for fools that be slippin then hit them for their shit. What kind of shit? Money, cars, clothes, dope, anything that we can make cash off! So you mean to tell me that all of this time; yall been stick up kids. Yep! Damn did Meesh know that? Hell yeah; how do you think he got all those easy licks? What you mean Sway? Tahiry; you need to get up on game shawty.

I stay on point Sway; don't get it fucked up! Oh yeah, then why didn't you know that Meshaw was selling hot dope. Half of his packages came from niggas we robbed. Man stop playing with me; he bought that shit with his own money. Yeah some of it but not most of it, he paid me and Skeet to do a few jobs for him. Wow; I could have been a dead ho if that info got out. Yep;

it almost happened a few times too but Meesh caught wind of it then smashed it.

See yall are too crazy for me! I sure hope you don't think I'm gone help you and Skeeta. In a way I do. How you think Sway? Well me and Skeeta got to thinking how profitable it would be if you and Kodi did steak outs for us. Dude what are you talking about, this aint no Law and Order. It's easy; yall tip us off about your rich tricks then me and Skeeta go rob them and split the take with you and Kodi.

It sounds easy enough but I'm not trying to get locked up! You're not gone get locked up Tah, by the time the cops get involved yall will be long gone. Did you speak with Kodi about this? Yeah she already helped us a few times before; you're just getting in the game so we're filling you in. Well, as long as Ko is down; I'm in. And Sway? Yeah what is it? No dead bodies man!

We're just trying to cash out Tahiry; that's all. I have a few questions though. What kind of questions? Are we robbing everybody or just the rich ones and do you break in houses too? All you need to remember is cash-out! If we can get paid off that trick; set his ass up! Ok and I don't have to be there; right? Nope all you do is set it up Tah. Cool, I'm in. That's what I'm talking about baby; now just sit back and follow along. We're about to bust this left on Fulton Industrial, I need to get this cash to pay my cell bill real quick. What are you talking about; follow along? Just be quiet and listen; you're about to learn something.

The sun has set and it's dusk over on Fulton. Sway rolls the Range down the strip doing about 20 miles an hour, observing several ladies walking up and down both sides of the street; dressed in revealing attire. Damn Swayzee; are these prostitutes? Yep; in the flesh! Sway blinks his head lights towards one of the girls as he makes a U-turn towards the Waffle House. She sees him then walks closer to the sidewalk as he approaches her. Roll the window down Tah and don't say shit.

Tahiry's eyes; now filled with doubt and excitement stretches wide as golf balls as the streetwalker approach her window. Hey Daddy; what's going on; this is a nice fucking Rover! Thanks; are you working? Yes I am; I aint out here with my ass and Titties hanging out for nothing. Her stringy blonde hair blew in the wind as cars and trucks zoomed by. Her double D breast set up perfectly; braced by her red push up bra and tank top. The ho's; flat stomach and nice hips; held up her Tru Religion jeans, no belt as she towered over the Rover window in her 6 inch red heels.

My name is Sharon, what's yours daddy? Is this your girlfriend sitting here all quiet? I'm Jeff and yes that's my girlfriend; Rachel. Well did you guys want to spend some money with this white whore or what? This is illegal you know; I can't be standing her too long now. Tah hastily places her right hand over her mouth. Yeah close your mouth honey; I call myself a whore all the time, that's what I am. So what's it gonna be Jeff; are you two in to some freaky shit?

I guess you can call it that! Trust me Jeff; I've done seen it all honey; what's your fantasy? Well Rachel likes to watch me getting head from another woman, it turns her on. Is that right; well I can do that for you, no problem. Do you have a condom Jeff? Sure, I got one. Ok let's do it? Hold on; how much do you charge Sharon and do you have a room? I charge $100 and I have a room but we can just go down the street and park behind that abandon hotel over there. My room is 5 miles that way, not unless you want to drive that far.

Damn Sharon; how long have you been out here today? Hell, since 10 O'clock this morning; I aint been back to the room since. Wow; is business good that time of day. Hell yeah it is; that's why I haven't gone back to the room yet. I'm scared I'm gone miss some more money. Well we don't want to hold you up any longer, behind the hotel is fine. Rachel; get in the back and let Sharon ride up front. Tah opens the door, exits then gets in the back seat.

Ok Sharon let's go have some fun; I hope this isn't weird to you. Honey please, this is normal; make a left right after this light then drive around to the back. Swayzee cruises onto the parking lot of the abandon building then makes his way around back, away from view of the road. Alright get your condom out, put the car in park, turn off the engine, roll down the windows and honey, you can slide up closer, so you can see me suck your man off!

Silently; Tahiry shakes her head to confirm as Sharon reaches in Sway's unzipped jeans, pulls out his hard

Johnson, sticks the magnum on top then commences to slide it on with her wet mouth. Damn Sharon that shit feels good! Umm-hmmm. Tah eyes stretches wide as she looks at Sway with discuss. He reaches under his arm rest with his right hand then pulls it back out. Click! The hammer drops on his 357 as the nose of the cold black steel; rest on Sharon's now, still dome.

Ok you know what this is Sharon, I want you to pick up your purse with your right hand and give it to me, now bitch! Here, here, take it, please don't kill me. Tahiry's forehead starts to sweat as she looks on, legs shaking repeatedly, heart pounding faster than ever before. Alright good girl! Here Rachel; take this

ANTWAN BANK$

and see how much money this whore
made for us today. Huh! Rachel; take
the damn bag and count the fucking
money! Oh, ok!

Sharon while she's counting; I want
you to take off all your clothes and leave
them on the floor. Ok whatever you say
sir! Call me Jeff; sir is not necessary. Ok
Jeff! She begins to remove her clothes as
asked; head still lying in Sways lap
while under the steering wheel, her legs
now up on the seat as she slides off her
jeans. Now sit up, take off that shirt-

It's $3,685.00 baby! Damn Sharon; you
was a good ho today! Do you smoke
Sharon? Yes I do Jeff! Good, now take
off that top and bra. Now Sharon! Ok,

ok, I'm sorry. Rachel; give me $5! Here you go! Thanks baby! Sharon, here's $5 for some cigarettes; thanks for the cash too, now get the fuck out! Oh and if I hear anything about you calling the cops, next time I'm gone leave your ass stinking. Remember I got your purse with your I.D Bitch! Rachel get in the front baby and let's get the hell out of here. Tah jumps out of the Rover, bypasses Sharon then jumps in the front as Sway is pulling off! Errrrrr! Sharon now in awe of what just happened; stands there flipping the bird as the white Rover speeds off the abandon lot. Fuck you Nigger!

Ring-Ring! Hello! Hey I'm calling about your ad on back page; is this

Kodi? Yes it is honey; are you law enforcement? No baby; I'm straight! Ok cool, how much time did you want to spend with me? Um about 30 minutes. Great but can you do me a favor? Sure; what is it Kodi? I don't have any condoms; can you stop by the store and pick up one before you come? Click!

Dammit; I knew that motherfucker was a cop! She shakes her head then places her cell phone back on the bed, lay across the end and continues to watch TV. Ring-Ring! Hello! Hey knuckle head; I'm about to stop by Church's Chicken; did you want me to bring you something? No Skeeta; I'm good baby; thanks for calling.

Tahiry

It's no problem, are you alright up at that room by yourself? I can park downstairs in the parking lot if you want me to. Not right now just stay close by though. I might need to do an outcall later. That's cool; you had any dates yet? Hell nah and the police called me about 2 minutes ago trying to act like a trick. No shit! Yep! How did you know it was a cop? I asked that trick to bring me a condom and he hung the fuck up.

Yeah Ko; that fool was a cop. Man, I'm really kind of shook now, after that. Do you have your gun? Always got that Skeet! Cool, well I'm gone get me some of this yard bird then I will head over

88

your way. That's straight; where are you going to be?

 I'll probably be over at Dudley's shooting some pool or something. It's only a few minutes from Panola rd. That's what's up; I'll call you if I need you. Alright; be easy Ko. Ring-Ring! Ring-Ring! Hello this is Kodi! Hey sexy; I'm calling about your ad; I'm tryna come see a bitch. Hold on; didn't you read the ad; it clearly says to be respectful! Oh my bad baby girl; that's just the way I talk. I didn't mean to offend you, but I do want to come through though; on the real; you feel me? You aint no cop; are you? Man fuck them police; I got's no love for em. Now what's up with the business? How much time are you trying to spend with me? I'm gone need that whole hour; you feel me. It's been a few weeks since I cut something; you feel me?

Well that's gone be $350; what time did you want to come by? Right now baby! Ok; I'm off Panola and I-20; call me when you get close. Shit that aint gone be long; I'm right off of Redan road. Cool, call me when you get by that Race track gas station. Ok, see you in a minute baby girl. Yeah; see you in a minute. Kodi walks over to the bathroom counter, retrieves two large white towels, places them on the other twin bed then removes her clothes, sits on the edge of the bed closes to the door. She faces the mirror then fixes her hair, stands up, puts one foot on the dresser, picks up the K-Y jelly then proceeds to lubricate her vagina and asshole.

Ring-Ring! Hello! Hey I'm calling about your ad. Yes baby how can I help you? Do you do fantasies? It depends; what's your Fantasy baby? Well it says on your ad that your name is Kodi; is that correct? Yes it is. Ok great; my daughter name is Kodi also and I was wondering if you would pretend to be her while I'm fucking you. What the hell; you sick bastard! Click! She throws her phone back on the bed then begins to talk to herself in the mirror.

"Lord; please help me out of this situation; I need me a man with some paper to take me out of this damn game." "I don't know how much longer I can do this; these men are crazy. Lord if you hear me, send me a sign please!" Ring-Ring! Hello this is Kodi. Hey I just pass Race trac and I'm pulling into the Burger King now baby girl. Cool take that road behind it and I'm in the very last hotel in the back. That's what's up; what room number. 352! Ok be there in second!

Ring-Ring! Hello! Bitch where you at? Girl, I'm in the room waiting on a new client, what's up? Child I called you to tell you what happened last night. What happened, Tah? Okay; remember I was supposed to go eat with Swayzee right. Yeah. Girl we ended up driving to the South side over on Fulton Industrial. Why the hell yall go way over there? Shut up Ko and let me tell you! Hurry your ass up then I got a date coming. Knock-Knock! Damn he's here. Knock-Knock! Tah; I'll call you after he leaves ok! Alright and don't forgot bitch. I won't! Knock-Knock! Kodi slips on her white robe then answers the door.

Hey! Hello baby girl; damn, you're ready huh? Yep; come in and make yourself comfortable. Alright baby. I'm Kodi; I didn't get your name. Oh; call me Tiger; baby girl. Tiger stood 6'3" tall, fair skinned with Shirley Temple curls hanging from under his Red Braves baseball cap, Red cargo shorts hung to his calves that met the top of his all black sweat socks. His red and white Jordan's matched his white T-shirt with the Red Atlanta letters across the chest. Where are you from Tiger? I'm from the Swats baby. Oh yeah; what brings you all the way to the East Side; you're a long way from South West Atlanta.

I'm over here on some business; you feel me? Yeah I guess; you can go ahead and take your clothes off though; I don't bite Tiger. Hold on before I do that; how much are you charging a nigga? What did we talk about on the phone Tiger! That's the price; if you don't have it; you need to leave. Hold on now baby girl; I just forgot; that's all. Well you can go ahead and put it on the table. I got you but want you go ahead and drop that robe, so I can see what I'm paying for; you feel me. Ugh; oh God! Against her gut feeling; Kodi now standing by the bathroom sink, drops her robe to the floor as he stands in front of the dresser watching. Damn; you're fine as a motherfucker girl. Yeah thank you; are you ready now?

Hell yeah! Tiger removes his shirt then unzips his shorts while Kodi gets under the covers. He sits on the opposite bed to remove his Jordan's while his back is to Ko. Alright sexy bitch! Oh fuck, what are you doing! Shut up and listen ho! Okay, Okay, just don't shoot! Calm as standing water, Tiger with both of his hands now occupying nine's, made sure he held them steady as he pointed them at her. This here; is my territory; you understand! Every ho on this block is mine. If you want to work on this side, you got to be on my team; you feel me.

I said do you feel me; bitch? Yeah I do; I do! Good now where's the damn money? It's in my purse! Where that shit at? Right there by the T.V! Tiger backs up to the T.V, picks up her Coach bag; then dumps the contents on the bed. Oh you need more than this ho; fine as you is and this is all you got. What the fuck a pimp gone do with $600! You need some motivation baby girl!

Kodi now nervous, gripping the sheets tight while clinching her knees to her chest sits there quiet and scared. Hey bitch; I'm taking this measly ass $600 to go buy me some Purp; when I get back, you better be on your back giving up that pussy or you better be gone! You feel me! Um-hmm! I said do you feel me ho! Yes Tiger!

Good, I'm taking this I.D too, just in case you want to act crazy. I can find your pretty ass. He throws the empty purse at her, puts his shirt back on then exits the room. Kodi jumps up then locks the door behind him and flips the silver latch over the back so no one could enter. She runs over to her suitcase that's sitting on the floor by the end of the dresser, pulls out her Browning 380 pistol and sits it on the bathroom counter. Ring-Ring! Hello! Hey Ko; I'm at Dudley's if you need me! Skeeta! Yeah baby, are you good? No; this pimp name Tiger just robbed me! Damn; I'm on the way; are you at the same spot as always on Panola? Yeah. Ok be there in a minute. Skeet! Yeah baby? Call me when you get in the parking lot; I might have a date because I'm still working; I aint letting that punk ass pimp stop my paper! Ok Kodi, no problem baby.

Kodi picks up the phone and makes a call. Ring-Ring! Yes hello! Hey Stanley; how are you doing Daddy? I'm great; is this my Kodi? Yes it is sugar; I want to see you today. I want to see you too baby; where are you? I'm working on Panola today; what time can you come? Well I need to stop by the cable company first then I can come by; so about an hour and a half. Ok that sounds good Stanley; I'll see you then and can you bring some gin? Sure sugar; see you in a few.

Ring-Ring! Hello! Hey is this Kodi? Yes it is? Ok I was calling to see if I can do a date with you? Who am I speaking with? My name is Jason. Hi Jason; are you affiliated with any type of law enforcement? No Ma'am. Hold up; how old are you Jason? I just turned 18 today and I wanted you to be my present. Oh really. Yes Ma'am. Ok let's stop with the

Ma'am's; call me Kodi. Ok Kodi. Thank you; now do you have any money Jason? Yes; I just got my check from McDonalds today. Oh how sweet but I'm sure you don't have enough. Your ad said $400 for an hour and $350 for a half hour. Yes it does; do you have that much Jason? I have $495! Well ok then sir; when did you want to see me? Sometime soon Kodi; I'm really excited!

You might want to calm down a little before you come see me. If you're still excited when you get here; that won't be good for you and I don't give refunds. Ok I'll calm down; can I come see you right now; your ad says you're working in Panola, Conyers, Lithonia and I-20 east. What does that mean Kodi? It means I'm available to customers that live in those areas. Where are you located Jason? Oh; I just got off work. I'm still sitting in my car at McD's on Panola. Oh really. Yes Ma'am- I meant Kodi. Do you have protection Jason? Yes; in my wallet. Good boy; well I'm in the hotel behind BK not far from you now. Cool!

So drive to the back and call me when you park, then I'll tell you which room I'm in. Alright I'm on the way. Oh Jason! Yes! What kind of car do you drive? A red, Volks Wagon Beatle; why? I'm going to be watching for you, that's all; did you leave yet? I'm pulling onto Panola now. Ok Jason; see you in a minute. Ko checks herself in the mirror to make sure she was ready. With her right hand she swings her robe open then rubs her pussy to see if it was still wet. The KY jelly from before had dried a little so she adds some more. Ko closes her robe, picks up her gun then places it under the pillow. Ring-Ring! Ring-Ring! She runs over to the window; cell phone in hand.

Ring-Ring! Hello; Jason? Yep I'm here. I know; I see you; that's a pretty car; did you just have it painted? Yeah my Dad got it painted for my Birthday. Aww, how sweet! Thanks, what room are you in Kodi? Oh I'm in 217; don't forget your protection Jason. I have it! Ok come on up. Jason; a slim, pale, white young man; runs up the cement steps then knocks on the door, his heart beating fast while he steadily keeps moving his sandy blonde hair away from his left eye brow.

With his right hand, he slaps against the door once more. Yeah who is it! A male voice yelled out. Oh, um, is Kodi in? Hell nah nigga; you got the wrong room! Nervously Jason steps back and looks at the numbers on the door. They read 215. Ahhh, I'm sorry sir! Yeah; get the fuck away from my door. The adjacent door cracks open then a female voice whispers out. Hey, what are you doing? That's not 217; come in here. Yes Ma'am. Call me Kodi, you are Jason, right? Yes.

Now with both hands in his pockets; her young client stands with his back against the door, rubbing his right Nike shoe across the top of his other foot as he nervously scans the room. Are you nervous; sit down and get comfortable; I don't bite; unless you want me to! Yes Ma'am. If you call me Ma'am again, we are going to fight. I'm sorry Kodi; this is my first time doing this. Oh relax; it's no different than all the other times you snuck a girl in your room. I never did that; my parents would kill me. They told me to wait until I was married. Hold up! You mean; you're a virgin? Yeah.

Ok you didn't say that on the phone; are you sure that this is how you want your first time to be? Yes! Alright; you need to sit down and relax because you had a hard on since you walked in. At that rate you won't last a minute with me. What do you mean by that Kodi? You're too excited Jason, just relax and get comfortable. Desperation followed by uncertainty could be seen on his face as his skin tone changed from pale white to red.

Kodi grabs his hand then leads him over to the bed. Now take off your T-shirt and shoes, just relax. Ok thank you. It's no problem, I have some cold beers; do you want one? No I'm not old enough to drink. Damn boy; you live a boring life, don't you! Ko reaches in the small fridge and pulls out two cold beers. Here drink this; it will help calm your nerves. As Jason sips on his beer; Ko removes his shoes, pants and T-shirt. So how much time did you want to spend baby; 30 minutes or an hour? I want an hour; well we can try but it probably won't take that long. So can I have a refund for the other 30 minutes if it doesn't? Ha-ha! I don't do refunds but we will work something out since it's your first time.

Thanks Kodi; you're cool. Oh I'm cool huh; let's get started, take off your boxers and lay back. Where's your condom? Oh; it's in my back pocket. Stop; lay back down; I'll get it. Ok you want me to put it on? No; I'll do it; you probably never even used one before.

Yes I did. For what- never mind, don't answer that; just relax for me. Jason now butt ass naked, dick pointing to the ceiling, waits patiently and intoxicated while Kodi removes her robe then slides closer to him. She rips open the condom, sticks it in her mouth then leans over his cock.

Kodi, don't swallow it! Shhhh. She motions to him with her right pointer finger over her pink lip glossed lips, rubber on her tongue. Ummm. He moans then grabs the edge of the bed as her warm mouth moves slowly up and down his young dick. Jason holds on tighter and tighter as she continues to perform fellatio on him. Ummm. How does that feel Jason? Umm- Umm-

Never mind; I'm gone go down on you for a few more seconds than we can fuck; ok. Umm, Ok.

Ugh! Ugh! Jason! Hold it! Hold it Jason! He holds on tight to the edge of the mattress as she jumps up then straddles him. Ko's perfect breast, flat stomach and flawless skin overwhelms him as she inserts his pony inside her womb. Alright Jason; stay focus for me baby! I know this pussy, feels good to you but try not to nut too fast, ok! O- O-Ok Kodi. Up- then down, back- then forward she went as slow as she could. Ring-Ring! Ring-Ring! Keep quiet Jason I need to answer this. Uh-huh. Ring-Ring! Hello! Hey Kodi; I'm in the parking lot baby; what room are you in?

Ok Stan; give me a few minutes to clean up; ok daddy! Sure no problem. Alright Jason it's time to cum baby! Kodi places her hands on his chest then proceeds to ride him but a little faster. Umm- Umm- Umm- What's happening to me? You're having an orgasm Jason; come on and fuck this pussy!

Umm- Umm- Damn baby; you got to stroke me better than that. I can't- My legs are shaking. What! My legs! Ko looks down and back at his legs. Wow; did you cum Jason? I- think so. Let me see! Ko lifts herself up then looks at the condom. Yep; you're done; here take this baby wipe and clean yourself off. Wrap that condom in some toilet paper and flush it please. Ok, thank you. Yeah you're welcome. Jason walks to the bathroom as Ko makes her way over to the bedroom sink. Did you flush it Jason? Yes. Good; come on, put your clothes on; I have another date coming. But aren't we going to talk or something? Boy talk about what! I don't know; something. Jason this is business honey; go on about your day. I need to wash up for my date.

Ok but what if I want to do it again? Do you have some more money? Yes but not on me. Ok you have my number; call me when you get it. I really need to get ready. Alright I'll call you later. Great, I'll be here! She picks up her cell then calls Stan as Jason closes the door behind him. Ring-Ring!

Hello! Hey Stan; give me about 10 more minutes; then you can come up. Sure thing baby which room are you in? Oh 217 honey. Ok see you in ten. Alright; see you in a few, big Daddy.

Ring-Ring! Yeah this is Kodi! Hey Ko; is everything alright? Oh hey Skeeta; yeah I'm straight. That pimp aint bring his ass back; did it? Nah; fuck that nigga! Well I'm downstairs in the car smoking on one, I'm going across the street to get some wings; call me if you need me. Thanks Skeet; I will.

Welcome to Wing Stop sir; what can I get for you? Yeah let me get 12 of those lemon pepper wings man, with some fries too. Did you want a drink too? Damn; don't it come with one? No it doesn't. Yeah, add A Lemonade! Alright brother that will be $9.67. Here you go. Thanks it will be ready in 15 minutes. Well; look who it is Flawless. Who you talking about Stallion? It's Skeeta, right there at the counter girl. Are you paying for our food too; Teddy Bear? Oh, hey ladies what's up! Man what happened to yall the other day? Yall lame for that shit!

Hold on Stallion; we got fucked up off that hydro and that was it! Yeah, yeah whatever, are you paying for our food or not? Sure Flawless; I got you, go ahead and order. Stallion what you want girl? Get me a large ice tea and one of those cheese steaks. Ok got you. Hello Ma'am, how can I help you? Yeah can I have one Philly cheese steak with a tea and one tilapia dinner with a coke? That's a Philly with an ice Tea and One Tilapia dinner with a coke. Yep that's it baby. Alright Ma'am, your total is $18.85. Alright; hold a minute; Skeeta I need $20. Oh here you go baby. Thank you Teddy Bear! No problem.

6 small oak wood tables, with two chairs each, line the window front that surround the lobby as the local radio station play over the speakers. Stallion sits on Skeeta's lap while Flawless sit in

the chair across from them. We were waiting for yall to call us the other day. I meant to call you Stallion but we were high and my home girl needed a ride over to Marietta that night. Damn you must be cutting that, you drove her way over there from the Deck! Nah she had to go see one of her regulars.

Oh, so your home girl is a ho! Stallion stop being mean! I aint being mean Flawless; he said it. Yeah you can say that Stallion, she works that back page shit. See Flawless! Shut up Stallion; she aint no different from your ass. You too bitch; don't even go there with me Flaw! Why she didn't drive herself out there Skeet; that ho fucked up our money. Because I'm her driver; that's why!

Don't tell me that you're a pimp Skeeta! I aint no pimp Flawless; she's my home girl and I look out for her. Yeah your ass a pimp nigga; how much she pay you to drive her? $75 sometimes 50, why you ask Stallion?

He aint no pimp Flaw; he's something like a pimp. Ha-ha. Bitch you crazy! Do yall work back page too? Hell nah man; we pick our dates up at the club, just like we met you and your boy Swayzee. Damn right, tell him again Stallion. Aint nothing wrong with back page, if that's your hustle, shit get money. Fuck that Skeeta, them ho's be on there tricking for 40 and $60, that aint no money honey; Flawless got standards!

That's not a bad hustle though Skeet, if you do 5 trips, you've made $375 in a day. It's ok Flawless. So what do you do for her besides drive her there, do you wait on her too? Yeah Stallion; I wait on her and if she needs me to beat a nigga's ass I will do that too. Ok that's what's up, so we can call you if we have a private party and need security? Yes you can Flaw; I got you. Alright but we aint paying you to do it though! Ha-ha. Then yall better not call me Stallion, I needs to get paid baby.

How about we give you head, anytime you want and you can cut one of us sometimes too! Nah Flawless, how about some head from one of yall and $50 for each trip but throw in an extra

$75 for private parties. Nah nigga we don't need you to drive us to no date; I'm talking about private parties where we need security. Ok Flawless, just throw me $200 and keep yall head and pussy.

Damn shawty; you a hard nigga to work with. I aint hard to work with Stallion, I'm just about my paper baby. I understand that but give us a break man. Ok girls; $125 and some head from both of yall. Stallion; get your Teddy Bear, this fool is crazy; the price is cool Skeet but you can only get head from one of us. Cool, that's a deal. Alright folks your food is ready, one Philly, Tilapia Dinner and Lemon Pepper wings with a Tea, Lemonade and Coke.

Tahiry

Alright bruh, appreciate it! Yep my pleasure! Here you go ladies! Thanks for the food Skeeta, what are you about to get into? I got business with Swayzee; yall got my number though just hit me up. Ok and you better answer the phone too, even if you're with that ho friend of yours. Stallion stop tripping, it aint that serious, just call a nigga! We will; see you later then Skeet!

Welcome to Café Intermezzo ladies; what can I get for you? Hey baby; give me a French Latte and one of your Duck Omelet's. Ok and for you Ma'am? Yeah I'll have a glass of Merlot and your Egg and Cheese Panini. Alright ladies; I'll be right back with your drinks after I put your orders in. Thanks Baby! Kodi; why in the hell did you order a Duck omelet, you're not gone eat it. Tahiry you know I don't waste no food girl; besides I had it before; it was pretty good. Alright I hear you. You got nerves questioning me and you ordered a glass of Merlot; 10 o'clock this morning.

Bitch I had a long night; I need a drink. Tah you aint did no fucking last night. How many trix you pull? I did three girl; that was enough; after I made that 1200 I was done. Baby you had an easy night; I fucked 8 niggas, got stuck up by a pimp and I still didn't get no sleep yet. Damn bitch; 8? Yes Tah 8, my damn stomach feels like a punching bag right now. Umm-Umm, you better than me

Tahiry

Ko and what you mean you got stuck up?

This old lame ass pimp named Tiger call like he was a date then when he got there he pulled out on me. That fool said I was working his turf and needed to pay him. Shit, why you aint cap his ass girl? He caught me off guard Tah, my gun was still in my bag. Damn that's messed up, he aint touch you, did he? Nah, he left after he took my money and said he was coming back but he never did. See, I would have been locked up or dead; I would have jumped on that punk. Tah, it's only money; I can make more. Kodi, you too soft bitch! Tahiry everybody aint crazy like you; I know your ass is certified loony. Whatever Ko!

Girl you ran over your boyfriend with your car then you were outside naked when you did it. What sane person does that? Fuck that Ko; he hit me. Here's your Merlot Ma'am and your Latte. Thanks baby. Like I was saying Tah; you got some screws loose. You damn right and when I see that punk who robbed you; I'm gone bust on his ass. Bust on him with what girl; you aint got no gun, bitch. No but you do and so does Skeet and Swayzee.

Tah drink your wine, you tripping over nothing. No it's not nothing Ko; what if he runs up on you again. You might not be so lucky. I hear you Tah but he aint gone do shit. Yeah ok; but just know I'm serious. It's too early for this where's my food? Don't ignore me Kodi; I'm serious. I know Tah; leave it alone.

Oh, I know what I had to tell you Ko! What now Tah? I had this client from Trinidad call me last night for an outcall. Anyway to make a long story short; I get to his room and he's already naked lying on the bed watching TV. I go through the whole spill and my rules then he throws me a curve ball. Surprised the fuck out of me! What he do Tah? He said there's an extra $200 on the dresser for you. I said thanks but why such a large tip, I just got here.

Kodi this man reaches under his pillow and pulls out a big purple dildo. Ha-ha!

Wow for real, niggas crazy bitch! Listen, so I go- why do you have that, do you want me to fuck myself with it? What did he say? This nigga says no; I want you to fuck me with it! Girl I was so shocked that I laughed my ass off. I think he got offended or something because he placed it in the drawer after I started laughing.

Bitch I would have stuck that motherfucker right up his Trinidad ass too. Noooo, I couldn't do it Ko! So did he take the $200 back? Well, after we talked a little I agreed to finger him in the ass. Ugh, did you wash your hands bitch! Yeah girl! He wants me to come back tonight and use the dildo this time. Are you going? Hell no; I'm not gone answer the phone. Shit, let me speak to him when he calls; I'll fuck that nigga.

No Ko; and why didn't you tell me that these guys were so damn freaky! Tahiry you aint seen nothing yet, just wait. Oh my God; I don't even want to know. Ha-ha! That aint funny Ko! Yes it is; with your high maintenance ass. Now that you have gotten your feet wet though. This is, easy money right? Yes it is Kodi; you were right; it's just dangerous but that's what makes it fun I guess. Girl that turns me on; the danger and the whole thought of me fucking a complete stranger; oh and the money of course. Seriously, we can travel to any city in America and do this girl. New York, Miami, Cali, anywhere. This is the life

Tah; sex, money, shopping, clubs and great restaurants, who can beat that?

I'm with you Kodi; I can't lie; I kind of like this life. Ladies here's your food; the Duck Omelet for you and Panini for you Ma'am. Thanks baby; umm, this smells good; you wanna try some Tah. No child; keep your Duck, I'm good.

"What's up motherfuckers; welcome to the world famous Flame." "Come out your God damn pockets and tip these strippers, twerking hard for them dollars." "This is yo boy; Dj Chi, get your money right. This next track is for my Dope Boys!" "Jeezy; My Hood!" "Let's go my niggas!" "We got Cream and Body on the stage and all table dances are $5; one time; The Flame, turn up!"

"Every time I do it, I do it for my hood" "And every time I do it, I do it for yo hood." "And every time I do it, I do it for they hood." "It's understood, I do it for the hood." Swayzee and Skeeta make their way through the club entrance which leads them in front of the bar as butt naked stripper's dance for customers along the walls, at tables and by the bar. Ones, Fives, Tens and Twenties fly in the air over the dancers as Hustlers, Dope Boys, Crews and Celebs shower the girls on stage while Jeezy's raspy voice penetrates the air. "And everybody on the block got the same agenda" "Hustle from January til the end of December" "Wasn't smoking purple, then it was more like Bobby Brown."

Yeah; it's turnt up in this bitch Sway! Hell yeah Skeet; this is my song right here though boy. Every time I do it; I do it for my hood! I do it for the hood! Alright young Swayzee; get me a Goose while you up here singing; I got next round. I got you shawty, go ahead and start scouting for some marks, check them ho's too; they getting money tonight up in here. I'm already on it Sway, you got the eye drops on you. Yeah it's in my pocket. Cool; I'll be right back; I'm gone take a walk around. Do yo thing bruh and look for them strippers with them garters on; holding that scrilla. You already know, they the first ones we ripping.

Hey baby; welcome to the Flame. What can I get you? Hey shawty let me get a double shot of goose on the rocks and a Jack Daniels and coke. Alrighty baby; that'll be $28.00! Damn yall expensive! Nah your ass is expensive; you ordering Top shelf. Well here's a 35; keep the change. Thank you baby! Umm-hmm.

Hey sexy, what's your name? Swayzee; what's yours? I'm Monay; did you want a dance? Nah I'm good shawty. Ok, why you holding two drinks? Oh this is for my partner; he went to the bathroom. That's what's up; what's his name? Damn, you kinda nosey; aint you ho? What! Fuck you nigga! Nah fuck you ho! Umm, whatever broke ass trick; let me go find a real nigga before I go off on your ass! Yeah that's right, keep walking, ol nosey ass; you need to do some sit ups!

Yo Sway! What it do Skeet; did you find something? Oh yeah; I got two fine ass shake dancers coming over on the next song. That's what it is; let's post up in this corner so we can hit the door after we jack them bitches. I feel yah Sway; here they come right now. Damn them sluts is fine as hell; did you check for the cash? Yeah both of em holding; one of them got their loot strap to her wrist tough. What about the other one? Hers is on her thigh.

Hey Skeeta; is this your friend that you told us about? Yep this is Swayzee; Sway this is Honey and Deja. Hello girls; what are yall drinking? Thanks Sway; we're drinking Remy tonight baby. Cool; hey bartender, can you get two Remy's; for Honey and Deja. Sure baby; coming right up!

Swayzee and Skeeta take a seat at the bar off in the corner near the exit and amidst the crowd as the ladies stand in front of them. Go ahead dance girls and don't stop until I tell you too. Damn Skeeta; you trying to kill us, aint you? No Deja; I just want to see yall sexy naked asses sweat a little bit.

"Alright motherfuckers; we're about to take this thing back!" "Once again this is yo boy; Dj Chi" "My girl Sky requested this next track; Go Dj by Lil Wayne." "Go Dj yeah that's my Dj." Here's your Remy's! Sway turns around then faces the bartender. Thanks, how much is it? $14.50! Girl; yall prices is fucking up your tip money; you feel me. It's all good baby I'm fine.

Sway reaches into the front right pocket of his jeans then pulls out the eye drops, leans over the counter, squirts a few drops into each glass of Remy then turns back around, drinks in hand. Here you go ladies; drink up and yall can stop dancing after this song, sit down and enjoy your Remy. Thanks! Yeah cool; no problem!

Honey I'm glad I came in tonight, it's crunk up in this bitch. I told you it would be Deja; your ass, just wanna stay at home up under your man every night. Girl; don't even go there. Here you go ladies; you can have our seats. Thanks Skeeta! It's not a problem Honey; drink your Remy and rest your feet because yall about to be dancing for the rest of the night. Shit, throw that money baby; we can dance until tomorrow if you paying. I know that's right girl; give me some! Deja raises her hand in the air to give Honey five. Smack!

Alright Deja; let's turn this up so we can get back to the money. The Flame, not really big in size had managed to fill with more people in the past hour, making it hard to move around. Now elbow to elbow, Honey, Deja, Sway and Skeeta find themselves trapped in the corner by the bar but right by the exit. The two stick up kids; stand in front of the ladies as they drink their spiked cocktails and wait on it to kick in.

Skeet; as soon as those bitches pass out, snatch that loot off Deja's garter and I'll get Honey's then break for the door. I'm on it bruh, they're about done now, it won't take long. Umm, that hit the spot; got my buzz on, you ready to make some more money girl? Thump! Zzzz!

Zzzz! Honey! Honey! Bitch wake your ass up! I can't believe this ho done went to sleep on the bar! Where's my phone; I have to take a picture of this shit. Deja looks on the bar and in her bag for her cell.

Damn it's getting blurry in here; I can't see nothing! Thump! Deja falls back in her seat then drops her head forward on the bar. Ok Swayzee; get that doe and let's break out fool. I got it shawty hit the exit. Skeeta and Swayzee hastily make their way through the crowd to the exit then out the front door pass the oncoming patrons. Yo, count that up Skeet; what you get? Hold on bruh; let me get in the car first. The fellas run across the street to the other parking lot then jump in the Rover, Swayzee in the driver seat; Skeet in the passenger's.

Yo I got $978 right here bruh. Hold on Skeeta; I'm almost done counting. Shit this is $1250 right here shawty. That's what it do; a quick two stacks, let's hit the I-Hop over on Panola by the crib. What you telling me for; you driving nigga; go ahead! Skeet; don't make me cut you up in this damn Rover. Swayzee you aint cutting nobody in this truck; you too scared you'll mess up the seats. Ha-ha! You got me there Skeet, call the weed man and tell him to meet us at the Hop. Which one? Call that Dred; his smoke is always on point. Alright; got you! Swayzee pulls off the lot, makes a left at the light then drives a few blocks down to the I-20 East exit speeding up interstate 20 at 80 mph. his tail lights disappearing in the distance as the jack boys make their way back to the East side of Atlanta.

3. No Risk; No Reward

Marietta, Ga.; Windy Hill Rd; Tahiry and Kodi find themselves amongst their counterparts competing for business. Cobb County police officers roam the highway for suspicious activity as dozens of tricks pull in and out of the hottest hotel on the strip. With its several floors, cheap rooms and easy access to Interstate 75; it's heaven for escorts, tricks, pimps and hustlers.

Come here Tah and look at this ad. Tah jumps off the twin bed and walks over to the table then looks at Kodi's lap top. So what do you think? Hold on; let me read it first girl. "Gentlemen, look no further, if you're looking for a good time with two upscale Companions; look no further. Ice and Mocha are here for your ultimate pleasure; all of our pictures are 100% real or your money back. So pick up the phone and call us now! Ask for the weekend double dip special!" "We are available for incall and outcall."

So I'm ICE and what is the double dip special? Yes you're Ice and I'm Mocha. Kodi your ass is crazy and these are not our damn pics. So what Tah; them fools aint gone say nothing about that! Look in the mirror; aint we finer than these ho's in the pics? Damn right bitch! Now what is the double dip special? Two bad ass bitches at the same damn time; tell that trick to put on a condom and dip his stick. Ha-ha! Ko you're a straight freak! Just make sure that trick changes condoms when he switches. Hold on ho, what you tryna say! Girl that's nasty, our juices mixing! Ewww! Whatever Tah, I need to make a run, do you want something from the store; I'm headed to the QT, we need to gas up. Yeah bring me a coke and some hot Cheetos.

Ok I'll be back in a few. That's what's up; close those curtains on your way out too. Umm-hmm; lay some fresh towels on the counter; oh and you said you wanted a coke right? Yes Kodi. A loud hum from the AC penetrates the now awkward silence as Tahiry walks over to the mirror to check her make-up, hair and dress. Mountain fresh air freshener mist the air, every ten minutes to mask the smell of cigarette smoke and God knows what else that lurked in the mid-price room. Dusty burgundy carpet cover the floor under the two twin sized beds that were draped with the same color comforter. One lap top, a white grocery bag full of magnum's, three Vanilla Visa prepaid cards and two prepaid flip cell phones sit on the dresser beside the retro boxed; 32" TV.

Ring-Ring! Ring-Ring! Hello! Yeah; I'm calling about your Double Dip special. Sure baby; are you law enforcement or affiliated with law enforcement in any kind of way. No baby; I'm not the police; is this yall's picture in this ad? Yes it is; how much time are you trying to spend with me and my girl? I was thinking more like an hour. Alright for both of us that will be $350 a-piece. Damn; that's $700! Yep and we're worth it too honey. I don't know about that baby; $700 is a lot of money for some ass.

Well if you want the best; it really isn't that much. You see the pictures; there really isn't any competition out there. Well which one are you? This is Ice! Oh, ok; you're sexy. Thanks; when did you want to come so we can get ready. I'll call you back Ice; let me think about this. Sure and what's your name honey? Jim. Ok Jim; call us back now! I will!

Ring-Ring! Hello! Hey girl; they got some boil peanuts up here; did you want some? No Kodi; I don't want no boiled peanuts. Alright don't get smart Miss Prissy; I was just asking. I wasn't; I just don't eat boiled peanuts. Well suit yourself; I'm about to pump this gas, be there in a minute; did we get any calls? Yeah one guy just called. Is he coming through? He wasn't sure about the price; he's gone call back. Umm; that aint gone happen; ok girl bye; see you in a minute! Ok Ko!

The loud sound of Kodi's stiletto's walking over the concrete towards the gas pump, along with her physique fitted in her tight jeans and black body top; attracted attention from every direction. She opens her car door, place the bags on the front seat then walks back to her gas tank- Excuse me Miss; can you spare dollar? He stood only 5'3", wearing dirty jeans, old Chuck Taylor's, a dingy white T-shirt and a head of hair that could be mistaken for a crow's nest. She looks at him with a soft heart then responds while reaching in her small purse that she held in her right hand. Sure baby; let me see what I have. Ko places the pump inside the tank then lets down the lever to fill it automatically.

She then opens her purse to retrieve her wallet as the bum looks on. Here you go- Buzz! Shit! You motherfucker; you fucking taized me! Kodi franticly holds the right side of her face in disbelief as the bum runs away with her purse while she screams loud as she could. Help! Help! He stole my purse! Somebody help! God dammit that fucker, taized me in the face! A few patrons stand and watch as he runs away, just as an officer pulls onto the lot. Hey officer! Officer; stop please! Kodi walks over to the car as he rolls down his window. Yes Ma'am; what is it?

This bum just robbed me at the gas tank then ran behind the store and through those woods. What did he look like Ma'am? He was short with a nappy head, a dirty white T-Shirt, dirty jeans and some old Chuck Taylor's. Was he a black male? Yep! What did he take from you? My damn purse with all my shit in it; and my motherfucking 380 was in there too! Alright Miss; I understand that you're upset but can you please refrain from using the curse words. Oh I'm sorry officer; my face hurts because he used a stun gun on me. Excuse me; did you say he used a stun gun? Hell yes, on my face; look at it! Do you want me to call an ambulance? No; I'll be ok; I just want my stuff back. We'll do our best to get it back for you Ma'am.

Yeah right; that shit is gone; I aint even getting my hopes up. Can you explain to me what happened from the beginning? Damn man; I already told you; wasn't you listening! Ma'am please- Stop calling me Ma'am; my name is Kodi! Ok Kodi; I'm gone need for you to calm down so I can get a police report. I'm calm sir. Good! The officer turns off his engine, gets out of the car then walks Kodi to the rear of the police cruiser. Have a seat on the trunk Kodi. Ko reluctantly jumps up on the trunk. Now let's start from the beginning.

Ok I walked inside the store to pay for my gas and picked up a few things. Did you see the accused when you walked in? No I didn't. Alright continue. So I walked outside to my car, placed the bags on the front seat, popped the gas tank, placed my purse under my arm then started pumping my gas. Is this when you first saw him? Nah I didn't even see him walk up. My back was turned when I heard a voice. What did you hear? He asked if I could spare a dollar. I looked at him, seen that he really needed it; so I said sure, click the pump lever on auto then looked through my purse. Then Bam! What happened then Kodi?

That dirty, stinky, motherfucker stuck a stun gun to my face! I screamed because that shit hurt like hell, that's when he snatched my purse and ran behind the building. My I.d; credit cards, gun and my money were in it. Did anyone see this happen? Hell yeah but they aint do shit; they just watched him run away. Alright Kodi; I'm going to call this in and get some more officers on it and have them search the area. In the meantime call your bank, credit card companies and report your things stolen so they can deactivate them. You can take this copy of the police report and get you a new copy of your license tomorrow. Ok thanks. Do you know the serial number on your gun? No but I have it at home in my safe. Good, here's my card; call me when you get that so I can add it to your incident report. Sure no problem.

I know you're still shook up but go home and try to calm down and let us handle this for you. Thanks officer; what was your name. I'm officer King. Thanks Mr. King! You're welcome

Ma'am; go relax and don't forget to call me when you get that serial number; I'm going to question some of these patrons to see what I can find out. Alright thanks again. No problem; just doing my job Kodi.

Ko makes her way back to the Charger, removes the pump, closes the tank, starts the car and heads back to the room. Frantic she picks up her cell then calls Tahiry. Ring-Ring! Hello! Hey bitch, guess what the fuck happened! Slow down Ko; what's going on? I got robbed girl, by a damn bum! What!

Yes girl! He stole my purse with my money, gun, id, credit cards; all that shit! This dirty motherfucker asked me for a dollar then taized my ass in the face. Oh no; are you alright? Yeah I'm good; I just filed a police report and the cops are on it now. Damn that's fucked up Ko; he didn't steal my Charger did he! No I'm driving back to the room now.

Alright hurry up; it's too much going on out there! I know Tah; this is crazy, I'll be there in a minute. Ok see yah in a bit Ko.

Ring-Ring! Ring-Ring! Hello! Hey Skeeta! Hey who is this? It's Flawless; are you home? Yep what's up? We need a ride to Douglassville. We who? Me and Stallion boy! Oh my bad yeah I'm at the crib; where yall at? Right here at the

Publix by your house on South Hairston. So are yall coming over or you want me to pick you guys up from there? You can come get us; we can leave our car here. Alright; I'll be there in a minute. Ok; I'll be waiting in the car, Stallion went inside to get something. Cool, see you in a sec!

Yo; I'll be back bruh! Where you going Skeet? I'm gone run Stallion and Flawless out to Douglassville to catch a trick. That's what's up; put them ho's down on that rip too. I don't know about that Swayzee; we don't know them like that. We'll test them and see what happens. Ok Sway I'll see what's up. Hey fill the truck up too! Yeah I got you! Thanks shawty!

Tahiry

As Skeeta pulls out of the apartment complex then onto Covington highway; he cruises down to the light at South Hairston; looks in the ash tray; pulls out a half of blunt; lights it while waiting on the traffic light to turn green then makes a left onto South Hairston then a quick right into the Publix parking lot. He immediately sees Flawless and Stallion leaning against the trunk of a dark blue; 740 BMW then rolls up beside them, slowly and let's down his window.

Damn; what's up ladies; yall looking sexy than a motherfucker! Hey Skeet; nice truck! Thanks Flawless! Hey Stallion; what's up? Aint shit; what's up with you nigga? I'm kicking it; smoking on this lil piece of blunt; yall ready? Yep; we're about to go see this rich ass Indian trick. Oh yeah! That's what's poppin; does he have a phat crib Flawless? It's huge Skeet but we mostly always meet him at this gas station in Douglassville. Gas station! Hell yeah. So; yall go to a room when he meets yall at the gas station? Sometimes we do. What you mean Flawless?

He's married; so we don't really go to his house but that fool got paper; he owns like three car lots and shit. Well if yall don't go to a room; where do yall go to handle business Stallion? Man we do it right there! Where, at the gas station? Yeah nigga; as long as that fool is paying; I'll fuck him at a car wash; you feel me! Ha-ha. Alright; I hear you Stallion. Well get in; let's go get that paper; I have to be back in the Deck by 9 tonight. Ok let me lock my car. Stallion gets in the front seat of the Rover as Flawless locks the 740. So how much are you charging us Skeet? You can just give me some head Stallion; I'm straight on paper right now. Alright nigga; don't get hook on this good Georgia Dome now. Ha-Ha! We'll see about that; I done had some good head in my day. That may be true but my head game is sick! I hear you Stallion.

Flawless opens the back door then jumps in the seat, purse and cell phone in hand. Ok I'm ready; let's roll out; what yall talking about? I was just telling Skeeta about how fire my head game is. Oh snap; don't get hooked Skeet! Man yall two are a trip; aint nobody getting hook. Where bout in Douglassville we going? My bad baby; take I-20 to exit 37.

Alright that's just 30 miles up the way; we'll be there in a few. So what's up with your boy? He's at the house Flawless; call him. Nah; I'll hit him up later; I got to make this paper real quick then we're going to work at Follies tonight. I heard Follies was turnt up now. Yeah; it's money in that bitch Skeet! How much you guys make a night in there? I made $1800 last time I worked and that was a Wednesday night. Damn Stallion; you made that on a Wednesday? Yep; it's turnt up Skeet!

I didn't work last Wednesday but I made $1300 on day shift last Sunday. Hold up Flawless; you said you made $1300 during the day shift. Yeah man! Shit; me and Swayzee need to check that spot out then. Oh; yall coming to drop some paper? Hell nah Flaw; we're going to scout. Scout what nigga; some ho's? Nah Stallion; some marks! I don't understand; what do you mean; marks? For a lick; somebody with paper! So you saying that you and Swayzee be jacking fools? You got it Flawless! That's fucked up Skeet; yall don't be jacking bitches do you? A mark is a mark, Stallion. Well you better not try that shit on us; I'll stab your ass in the chest nigga. Ha-ha! You crazy Stallion! You damn right; I aint playing either Skeet!

We wouldn't do that to yall Stallion; you girls are cool with us but you two can get in if you want. Oh that's why you were asking us about this Indian; we're going to see? Huh Skeet? What you say Flawless? You heard me! You right but I still need to get some more information on him; you feel me. How much is our cut; if we help you? Shit; we can do 60-40 Stallion. Man you crazy; we're setting everything up; who get 60; not you!

Yeah we get 60 Flawless; me and Sway will be taking on all the risk; all you and

Stallion will be doing is setting him up.
Fuck that; what if we want more money.
Then get us some more marks Flaw!
Let's see how this move goes with this
Indian first Skeeta then we can talk
about that some more. Alright girls; I
can work with that; time to get your
game face on now though; here's the
exit.

Alright be quiet Skeet; let me call him.
Go ahead Stallion; handle your
business. Ring-Ring! Ring-Ring! Hello!
Hey big daddy; I'm like a minute from
the gas station; are you there yet? No;
not yet; maybe in two minutes. Ok that's
cool; what kind of car are you driving
today? A black Suburban with dark,
tinted windows! Oooh; are they really

dark, so no one can see us inside. Yes. Umm-hmm; I like that daddy; are you parking in front of the store or at the pumps? I want to park at the pump this time; I'm going to put the pump on auto then wait in the car for it to fill up while you're giving me head. Umm, daddy; you're a bad boy!

Yeah I know and if you don't make me cum before the pump stops; I won't owe you anything; can you do that Stallion? Of course I can daddy; my Georgia Dome is fierce! Ha-ha! Ok whatever; we'll see. So what do I get when I make you cum before the pump stops? I'll give you $500. Well; hurry your ass up; I'm here now waiting on you. Ok be there in one minute. Great; see you in a minute daddy!

Stallion; your ass is a freak! Flawless; I know you aint calling me no freak, when your ass is worse than I am! Yall crazy! Nah Skeeta; Flawless is a freak. Hey that's you guys business. Ring-Ring! Hold on; this is him. Ring-Ring! Hello! Hey I'm at the pump. I see you sexy; here I come; let me get my purse. Ok I'm going to start the pump. No; wait until I get in the truck; don't be cheating now! Alright; I'll wait. Thank you; here I come!

Damn; ol buddy is weird aint he? Hell yeah but that's right up Stallion's ally, she weird too. So what about you

Flawless? What about me? Are you a freak? Man, I just like to cum, get that massive orgasm; know what I mean; what girl doesn't. I feel you on that shawty but why you got to trick to do it? Skeet I've been doing this since I was 12 years old. Damn, for real; how old are you now? 29 and I'll be 30 this August. How the hell did that happen; I didn't know girls could cum at 12!

Every woman is different but for me; it was my next door neighbor. He used to always take me to the park with him while he played with his friends. Jacob was two years older than me; so my mom trusted him to look after me; her baby girl. Well to make a long story short; we always played hide and seek in the park.

One day I was trying to find a hiding spot and I accidently walked up on Jacob while he was taking a piss behind the building. When I saw it; I just stood there because I never seen one before; never; not even in my books, on TV, nowhere. He caught me looking then asked me if I wanted to hold it. What did you say? I said sure, then I walked over and he placed my right hand up under it and I held it in the palm of my hand.

It felt all soft at first, then it started to grow, bigger and bigger, harder and harder. I was mesmerized; I wanted to play with it forever; it was so beautiful, dark like chocolate, yet strong and full of life. Damn Flawless; that shit really turned you on; huh. Shut up Skeet and listen. Ok my bad, go ahead. Anyways; Jacob tells me that it taste like chocolate and asked me to lick on it and see. Did you? I did but it didn't taste like chocolate; he told me to lick it some more but to get on my knees so he could put it in my mouth the right way; like he saw his brother do to his girlfriend. He said that was the only way that the chocolate filling would come out.

So I licked it and licked it, sucked and sucked like it was a purple popsicle; my favorite. Jacob started to moan and groan then tensed up and grabbed my head and held it still. That's when it happened, something warm came down my throat and it tasted like strawberry milk, the kind my mom always fixed us before we came outside to play. Damn Flaw; that was fucked up how he played you. Did you tell on him? Nah; I sucked on his popsicle every day the whole summer until he showed me what my vagina was for. Once I felt his popsicle inside me; I wanted all the popsicles. Jacob would tell his friends and they would give him their allowance just to stick it in for two minutes. Wow, that's deep. I know and I've been tricking ever since.

Hum, I see it got you hard; you ready for some of this Georgia Dome? Hell yeah; let me get some; hold on I need to take out my popsicle! Ha-ha! Fuck you Skeeta; let your seat back and move up that steering wheel. Skeeta turns up the AC in the Rover, lock the doors, roll up the window then leans the soft leather seat back as Flawless places her soft juicy lips on his cock. Skeeta, let me know if somebody is coming; keep your eyes open nigga. You know I'm bi-polar; you don't want me freaking out. Yeah umm-hmm, I got you; go back down.

Slurp-Slurp! Damn girl; you're a motherfucking professional, suck this popsicle! Um-hmm, suck it bitch, suck it. Ring-Ring! Ring-Ring! Damn; your phones ringing but it can wait; go ahead and finish. Ring-Ring! Ugh don't stop;

let it go to voicemail. Ring-Ring! Just chill Skeet; it's my nigga, don't say nothing and turn down that radio. Shit, alright handle your business. Ring-Ring! Hey baby; what's up; I was just telling Stallion about your new bike. I'm good, where you at though? I'm over at the Jamaican joint getting some curry goat with some rice and peas; you want something?

Nah, I'm good; they just called me in to work; I was just calling to let you know that I wouldn't be home tonight when you get off from the club. Ok thanks, that's what's up; be safe at work and I love you. Love you too and tell Stallion I said what's up. Ok babe will do; bye, bye.

Now can we finish? Nope you had enough, let's talk about that business. What business? The lick nigga! Oh we just need your Indian's home address and the car lot too; he probably has a stash there too. Cool; we got all of that already and Stallion even has one of his credit card numbers too; he paid for a room a few weeks ago and the lady at the front desk let her charge another day to it and gave her the bill with all his American Express info on it.

Damn, that's what's up right there. Yep the dumb bitch thought she was his wife. Did yall use it yet? Hell yeah; we went to Lenox and got us TRU Religion's the other day. Yeah he's a good mark; we gone set this up proper; you feel me. I feel yah nigga; just don't forget to break us off. Oh no doubt; we got yall, for sho. Man what yall in here talking about? Damn girl are you done already? Yep; that was a quick $500; that fool came so good he didn't even hear the pump stop. I heard that shit and just kept going like I aint hear nothing. That's my bitch right there! Get that doe baby! You damn right Flaw, you know how I do; now let's get over to Virginia Avenue; I have a new client waiting on me; you know strangers make my pussy wet.

Man yall two are some characters! Why you say that Skeet? I'm just peeping the scene, that's all Stallion. Well drive while you're peeping; we got an hour and a half before we need to be at Follies. I know that's right Stallion; we aint trying to pay no late fees. Hell no Flaw; you know we don't hustle backwards, we stacks the bread. Can we smoke some purp in here Skeet; I gotta get my mind right for tonight.

Yeah go ahead Flawless; yall good. Thanks baby. So did yall talk about this lick? Yeah I told him the run down on him Stallion; they gone set it up. That's what's up shawty; don't forget to pay a bitch Skeet. Hey it's all real, you feel me, yall good. Ok I was just checking; don't think we won't come shoot yall shit up. It aint even like that Stallion and I'm sure that yall would. Alright as long as you know, that's all I'm saying! Pass that purp Flawless; let a bitch hit. Flaw inhales then releases her smoke slowly while speaking. Here you go Stallion. Preciate it girl! Let's get out of here Skeet!

"What's up A-Town!" "It's a warm day out and I know yall about to shine up them whips baby." "Keep it lock right here to Power 99 and I'm going to keep these tunes bumping baby!" "This is yo boy Shi-C!" "Shout out to them trappers on the Eastside getting it in!" "This next one is for my girl Kodi out there getting her hustle on." "Here's Look at me now with that Busta Bust, Lil Wayne and Chris Breezy!"

"I don't see how you can hate from the outside of the club" "You can't even get in" "Hah-aha leggo!"

"Yellow model chick" "Yellow bottle sipping" "Yellow Lamborghini" "Yellow top missing" "Yeah, yeah"

Hey bitch, you need to get this paper tonight! What you talking Tiger, I made three stacks last night! Exactly ho! The mark is 5, so your ass is short. Man you crazy; you go out there and suck and fuck then! Bap! What you say ho! Bap! Oucccchhh; stop Tiger! You better watch your mouth or I'm gonna slap your trifflin ass again. Now pull out that I-pad and go to back page, so I can see what the comp look like.

That's all you had to say Tiger; you don't have to keep hitting me. If you just listen and stop talking back Desire; I won't have to smack your dumb behind. Now do what I say and find the ads.

Tiger turns the radio up just a little, leans back in his all black leather seat of the Chevy Avalanche as she search back page for escort ads.

"I get what you get in 10 years, in two days." "Ladies love me; I'm on my Cool J." So what's the word Desire; there any freaks I need to go check? Yeah daddy; I see a few new ones. Well how much they charging gurl? One of them got $40 on here and the other got $60. Let me see; are they fine?

Desire brings the I-pad closer to Tiger so he can see the ad post. Yeah that one for $40 is alright. Call that number for me, so I can go pay her ass a visit. Ok! Where is she posted? She has College Park and Virginia Ave. Yeah call her, she out here renegading and shit! Hold on, I'm calling her! Hey; watch your voice bitch!

Ring-Ring! Here Tiger; it's ringing! Ring-Ring! Hello! Hey I saw your ad on back page; I want to come through. Ok; are you affiliated with law enforcement of any kind? Nah; I aint no police! Good, how much time are you trying to spend? Your ad says $40! That's for a quick stay baby. What's that? 15 minutes! Hell that's all I need. Alright; I'm in a hotel off Virginia Ave in College Park. Cool I'm not far from there. Alright; call me when you get by the Chicken spot then. Ok gurl, see you in a bit. Alright baby.

Desire; reach under that seat and hand me my 357. Are there bullets in it? Yeah gurl but the safety is on. She carefully reaches under the seat as Tiger starts the Avalanche and cruises towards Virginia Avenue. Here you go daddy! Thanks; put it right there on the seat. You're not going to shoot her; are you Tiger? Nah, just scare her ass a little bit then get my money.

Money! Boy your ass is crazy; that girl don't owe you no money. Look; this here is my turf and any bitch that's getting paper over here gots to pay a pimp. Now shut up before I smack you again for talking too much. As a matter fact; write the number down for the other ho you saw on back page that's charging $60. I already put it in my phone.

Good; now just chill while I handle this business. But you just said that the East side was your turf last week! Bitch; the ATL is my turf; now shut the fuck up! Desire shakes her head, leans back and looks out the passenger window as they cruise down the interstate.

After several exits; Tiger pulls up to the light, just before the Chicken joint then redials the number. Ring-Ring! Hello! Yeah; I'm by the Chicken joint. Okay I'm at the six just behind the liquor store. Alright; which room are you in gurl? 430! Ok be there in a minute.

Tiger makes a right turn beside the restaurant then drives slowly pass each section until he reaches the 400 section. Aite Desire; stay here until I get back and keep the truck running! He tucks the chrome 357 in his pants, just in the small of his back. Be careful daddy and don't hurt her. Bitch you just be quiet and stay here, I got this! Bam! Tiger slams the door, runs up the steps and heads to room 430. Knock-Knock!

The curtains slide back just a little as he continues to knock then the door opens. Hey how are you? A female voice sounds out as she stands behind the door, hiding herself from view as he enters. Damn gurl; why you all behind the door and shit.

I'm just being careful baby; that's all. Ok I can dig that! Damn you've been fucking up something; aint you! Tiger blasted out as he scanned across the dingy hotel room. At least; a dozen gold, empty magnum wrappers, lie atop the filled small waste basket that sat just at the edge of the twin bed, closest to the door. Yeah you must have that good-good, gurl! Ha-ha! Why you say that baby? Hell I'm just looking at the pile of nasty white towels that you got stacked in the corner and all those damn magnum wrappers. Yeah, you're getting it up in here!

I do alright; you can put the donation on the table baby. Then go ahead and get comfortable. So, where are you from gurl? I'm from Chicago baby! Oh they got some good pimping up there, who's your daddy? I aint got no pimp and don't need one. Now did you want to fuck or not baby, I don't have all day, I have more customers waiting. Tiger pauses, smiles, reaches behind his back then quickly pulls out the 357. Oh my

God, hold on; what are you doing! Please don't shoot me! I aint gone shoot you bitch but I will take your cash. So come on and cash out ho!

Ok, ok I'll give it to you, just don't hurt me! Well BITCH here's the situation, I'm that smooth playa they call Tiger and all this turf is mine, here in the ATL. You got two choices! What are you talking about? Bap! Shut up and listen ho! The ho; now stunned from the stinging sensation that Tiger's right palm left on the side of her face, looks up at him with the fear of God in her eyes. As I was saying, you got two choices. Pay me and get on my team and make this money for me or get the fuck out of the A!

Now nervous, scared and mad as hell, she reluctantly goes in the drawer and gives him her hard earned cash. How much is that bitch? It's 8 thousand. Damn, you're an ATM, aint you! Alright let me have it! Tiger grabs the loot, stuffs it in his pockets then waits for her answer. So have you made your mind up ho! My way or the highway, what's it going to be?

Well if I'm gone fuck with you, I got to be the bottom bitch. Bap! Ho you don't make the rules! This is how it's going down; I'm going to run a few errands and when I come back here; you need to have some more money or be ghost! You got that! Umm-hmm. Bap! I said; you got- I heard you, dammit, stop slapping me! Good, I'll be back in a few hours then! You better have at least three stacks or I'm whipping that ass! Now trembling with a face full of tears, she shakes her head to confirm then stands there in awe as he exits the room shouting. Damn right, this here is Tiger's turf and don't you forget it!

Man Swayzee; this aint no kush my nigga. It's that midget Skeet but it's straight. Bruh that shit gives me a headache. I'm about to go over to the corner store to cop some loud from partner. You can let Kodi and Tahiry smoke that garbage. Pass me that blunt Sway; I'll smoke it! Yeah I already know that Kodi! Ko looks up at Swayzee with a smart look on her face as he hands the blunt to Tah. Ha-ha. He's calling you a weed head Ko! Tah fuck Sway punk ass; he's gone smoke some too.

You damn right Kodi; hurry up and light that! I'm lighting it boy hold on. Skeet; you aint gone yet! Wait too long and lil shorty won't be up there. Yeah I know Sway. Tahiry, Swayzee and Kodi all kick back on the couch while the TV's watching them as they pass the chronic from right to left as smoke fill the small two bedroom apartment space and its effects began to sink in. Tahiry stands up then paces back and forth while holding her head down.

Hey bitch; are you ok? I'm good Ko; just thinking about this plan girl. We need to come up on some paper; a bitch got bills and a shopping habit to support. Well Skeet put me up on this Indian Car salesman; out in Douglassville. What's that supposed to mean Sway? That fool is rich shawty and these two ho's we met at the Pin, tricks with him every week. That's a lick right there Sway; when are we doing it? Hold on Tah; I didn't say that you girls were helping. So why did you bring it up then Sway? I told you I'm on a mission for this paper nigga!

I hear you barking Tahiry but you damn sure looked spooked the other night while I was jacking that white ho. That's because it was my first time but I'm all in now; I promise you that Sway.

Yeah; my girl aint no punk Swayzee! Well your ass need to take some lessons from her then. That pimp; punked your ass out of all your paper. Man whatever, that fool had a gun and plus he caught me off guard. Don't worry about that faggot Kodi; we'll get that fool one day; he's bound to slip up. Yeah I know Tah!

You girls crazy; yall swear yall some gangsta bitches. If you two want some paper; place some ads on back page to attract those rich tricks, set them up then me and Skeet will go rob their asses. That's easy to do Sway but how much are we going to get for setting them up. Shit we'll give you guys a nice cut, make it worth it, you dig. Alright we'll do some outcalls to the rich neighborhoods and if the house is all that. Me or Kodi will text you and Skeet the address.

Now; that's a deal right there ladies! See and you thought that we were useless. I didn't say that Tah- Yeah whatever Swayzee; it's all good baby; just make sure we get paid. Oh for sho! Come on Kodi; let's place these ads girl; I seen some new Red bottoms I want. Bitch you is stupid; I'm trying to get that new Benz. That's you Kodi; I love my charger the Benz can wait!

Sway let me hold your lap top man so I can post this ad. Sway inhales a long pull from the mid, exhales then reaches under the couch and pulls out his lap top. Here you go Tahiry; make that ad sexy as hell too; yall should put some sexy ass pictures up with it. Man we got this; do what you do! Alright Kodi; I'm just saying.

Skeeta makes his way through the pathway then up the hill to the corner store where his partner stood posted. A frail gentleman with outrageous facial hair, dark dry skin and long arms, greets him as he gets closer. My nigga Skeet, what it do baby? What up partner; I need some of that loud; boy. You know I got you man; what you spending; 40? Yeah 40!

The frail drug dealer; reaches under the Newspaper stand that sits right outside of the store entrance and pulls out a purple plastic baggie. Here you go Skeet; tell that nigga Swayzee to get at me! Alright I'll do that and good looking out dawg! Ring-Ring! Oh shit let me get this. Hey my man; be easy. See you tomorrow! For sho Skeet! Ring-Ring! Hello! What's up Skeeta? What up; who's this? It's Flawless nigga! Oh my bad baby; new phone. Yeah save that lie; what's the word on the Indian? Baby we're waiting on you and Stallion to drop the address so we can go get that fool.

Well you need to talk to your boy; Stallion just texted Swayzee the address five minutes ago! Ok then that's what is Flaw; I'm on the way back to the house now. Alright call me and let me know something and don't try and jack us out of our cut either nigga. Flawless, stop with all-that girl; we got you, 100! Ok I hear you; bye then. Bye Flaw. Skeet makes his way back over the beaten path, down the sidewalk then up to his apartment door.

Damn shawty; it took you long enough! Kiss my ass Sway; I aint see your ass going to the store. Ha-ha! Kodi, Tah; what yall laughing at; aint shit funny. It's funny to meet Skeet! Ko your ass is just high; you'll laugh at anything. Fuck all that Skeet; where's the loud playa?

Calm down Swayzee; I got it but guess who call me though? Who bruh?

Stallion and Flawless; she said they just texted you that Indian's address! Oh yeah she did, when are we hitting that fool up? Stallion said he's going to Vegas for the next few days. So let's hit that joint tonight then Skeet. Man that's fine by me; I stay ready pimp. Hold up; what two bitches yall talking about and how they get in on our action?

Tahiry sit your ass down, I got control of this situation besides your ass is new to the game. You don't have no say in the matter. What fool; you a dammit lie! Tah sit down girl, them ho's aint got nothing to do with us. See Kodi; that's why I'm about to run shit up in here. All three of yall got the game messed up.

Bitch, sit your church girl ass down before I kick you out of my apartment.

Oh you don't have to kick me out Sway! I got my own shit, remember nigga! Tahiry please stop following Swayzee's ass up! Fuck him, Kodi! Skeet, is this the address right here! I saw it earlier but didn't recognize who sent it. Is it 4300 Robert Circle? Yep! Cool that's the lick then, we got two full nights to make it happen.

So you two fools are really going through with this job and yall don't even know these two skanks. They're cool Ko; aint no bullshit. How do you know that Skeet? Because, I'm the one that drove them to meet the Indian trick a few weeks ago! We've been planning this girl. Well go handle your business then nigga, me and Kodi are leaving! Hold on Tah- Bitch let's go, we have some money to make; my phone has been ringing ever since we placed that new ad.

Alright Sway; yall be safe! Ok Kodi! Bam! Damn Swayzee what's wrong with Tah? Man that girl is crazy; slamming doors and shit! I don't know Skeet but let's get ready for this job shawty. Did Stallion send some pictures of the Mansion, Swayzee? Hold on; let me check man. Yeah; she did send some! Hell, that jump off might be alright. Sway, that's a full fledge whore my nigga; aint no secrets; she don't even qualify to be no jump off man.

Whatever Skeeta; you know what the hell I mean. Man just look at these pictures so we can know what we're walking into. Swayzee walks over to the kitchen table; puts down his cell then scans through the photos of the huge brick mansion. Large crescent windows, cascade over the top half of the home allowing all to see inside through its clear glass panes. Caramel, marble floor tiles blanket the bottom floor as cream carpet cover the stairway. Gold, Lion statues, Vase and yellow roses accent the décor.

Shit Sway; there's some cash in this one for real. Yep let's get him; I want all the loot Skeet; even pennies, nickels and dimes. Bruh you're going to hell; God don't like ugly. God! God; Skeeta just shut up and put on your black clothes so we can go get this over with. Sway chill; that will only take a minute. As Skeeta walk to his room to get dressed, Swayzee takes a seat on the couch, places his 357, Nine Millimeter and Sawed off shotgun on the coffee table. The voices of Fred Sanford and Lamont play in the background as he starts to dismantle his Nine to clean it for later.

Hey shawty hurry your ass up; we need to be leaving. I'm almost done Sway; I need to put on my boots. Alright and don't forget your gloves this time boy! Oh; I already got them. Yo Sway we forgot to go see Truck and Nook about Meshaw's paper! Man, forget them chumps; I'll be in the Range, let's go get this loot! I'm coming, let me grab this Jeezy cd! Swayzee dressed down in black cargo pants, gloves, boots, black tee and black ATL fitted; sit in the Rover with the AC blasting as Skeet makes his way out.

The smell of fresh leather, fill the air inside the Range mixed with Kush smoke from Sway's blunt. You ready shawty? Yep; let's do it! Put that Jeezy in then, time to get money boy! Skeet slides the cd in the deck; blast the volume then takes the blunt from

Swayzee as Ballin kicks the Bose surround system of the cocaine white Range.

"You think you're ballin cause you got a block?" "He think he ballin cause he got a block" "You know these hoes came to see me ball" "You know these hoes love to see me ball." Alright so how are we rolling up on this crib Sway? Man we're just gone walk in that bitch! Oh you got jokes! Nah Skeet; Stallion texted me the security code! What! Say word, boy! No bullshit Skeet; she did that. Damn, we got to keep them ho's on team bruh. I already know; that was some real shit. Hell; fine as her ass is; she should be able to get all of them tricks like that.

Skeet I'm with you on that shawty. So where's the alarm pad on the house? She gave me the code to the one by the garage. Swayzee this is too easy, you sure this aint a set up? Hell nah; them ho's about this life; believe that. Alright I hear you; I know we better not end up in the pokey with Meshaw's ass.

Skeet you're paranoid, give me that damn blunt, and get your mine right too. We're just a couple of miles away from the spot. I stay ready boy; let's just get in and clean this rich fool out. Did Stallion say anything about a safe or some cash stashed in that motherfucker? Hell nah; we're on our own with that one Skeet. Sway brings the Range to a slow roll as he approaches the huge stone faced Mansion.

Damn this shit is huge bruh! Hell yeah it is, which damn garage door is it? Just pull up to the first one Swayzee. A row of 5 double car garage doors sit juxtapose to the main entrance at the end of the cobble stone driveway. As the sun set and dusk settle over the Atlanta skyline, Sway places the Rover in park, gets out and walks over to the garage door to access the key pad. Skeeta sat patiently in the passenger seat watching as the door, slowly rise.

Skeet; look at that player, easy as taking candy from a baby. Yeah come on; now let's get to work, back this fucker in, so we can load it up. Shawty you already know what it is. Alright I'm getting out so we can get a head start! Why you rushing Skeet; the nigga out of the country. Man anything can happen, I'll wait by the door while you back up. Ok put your gloves on.

As the garage door slowly comes down, Sway turns off the truck, pops the rear gate, inserts Travis Porter's cd, then joins Skeeta as they both enter the Mansion while the sound system plays in the background. "We in Kamal's" "I'm finna ball on em" "Magic City, we goin hard on em" "Strokers, we goin crazy" "One time for my independent ladies."

Alright shawty, you go hit the bedrooms upstairs and I'll get downstairs. Don't get no bullshit either Skeeta, only the expensive things. Bruh chill; I know what to get! Cool, meet me back down here in 30 minutes. Sway; that fool is out of town, why the rush! Ha-ha! You funny, let's just play it safe and be ready to go in 30; grab some pillow cases to wrap the shit up in too. Yeah, yeah I got it; while you're worried about playing it safe, you need to turn off that damn radio.

Man, just hurry your fat ass up! Whatever Swayzee; we going to Onyx after this lick too! That's cool Skeet, just get busy my nigga. Skeeta nods his head then heads up the bronze rail stairway to savage anything of value from the extravagant mansion. Sway makes his way into the kitchen striding over the caramel marble tiled floors; empties out the trash can then proceeds to clean the silverware from the drawers by dumping them into the empty garbage-pale.

He scrambles through the cabinets, top then bottom to no avail. Then in frustration pulls several plates; one after another from the cabinet then slams them against the tile floor. God dammit; all of this bullshit, where the fuck is the money! He pulls out his cell then calls Skeeta. Ring-Ring! Yeah what up! Man did you find anything up there; aint a damn thing down here. Yeah I just came up on a watch collection; he got some good ones in here too Sway! That's what's poppin; get that shit, I'm gone check the living room.

Why you ask, you aint get nothing yet? Hell nah, just some funky ass silverware! All of it adds up Sway, put that stash in the trunk then grab those pictures off the wall; they have to be worth something; look at this place! Shawty I don't care what nobody says about you, you do use your brain sometimes nigga. Sway, kiss my ass and get them flix bruh! I'm on it; don't worry!

Bet it up; see you in a few! Sway grabs the trash can, drags it to the garage then places it in the back of the Range as the music continue to echo in the garage. "You wanna see some ass" "I wanna see some cash" "Keep dem dollars comin" "And das gonna make dem dance." "Make it rain trick, make it rain trick!"

Sway slides the can to the side then heads back inside to grab the paintings off the walls. Ring-Ring! Ring-Ring! Man what does this ho want! Ring-Ring! Hello! Hey Swayzee; what's the business? Hey Flawless; we're still in here, so far; all we have is some watches and some funky ass silverware. Where the fuck is the cash at shawty! That trick is always talking about keeping his money close to him, did you check the bedroom? Yeah Skeeta is upstairs now.

Hmmm, oh check his office; it's in the far left corner of the house. Oh yeah; what makes you think that something is in there?

Whenever he sneaks me in the house; we're always fucking in there. I'm almost certain he stashes his cash in there somewhere because we drive straight there from the car lot and he always has the money on him. Well, your bow legged ass is gonna stay on the phone with me until I find something. This better not be a dud ass trip. Trust me Sway; there's something there baby. Ok we're about to see.

Soft white bulbs, barely light the long narrow hallway, spotlighting the

Picasso's, Basquiat's and Monet's that decor the walls. Damn Flawless, this dude has some serious paintings in this bitch. Let me call you back; I'm about to put these in the Range. Alright, didn't I tell you nigga! Yeah, yeah, I'll call you back in a minute. Ok Sway. Hastily he places the cell phone in his pocket then proceeds to remove the art pieces one after the other, loading them into the truck. What up bruh, what you get? Hey Skeeta; we got some famous art shawty; it has to be worth something, there's shit in here from Monet, Picasso and Basquiat! Dude I don't know what the hell you're talking about; can we get some cash for it? Hell yeah shawty! Alright then that's all I care about.

What you get from upstairs? I got these watches and a few diamond ear rings. Let me see those time pieces! Skeeta places a bed sheet on the floor of the truck, unrolls it then reveals the watches. Ok I see some Movado's, Cartier, a few Rollies and what's this one? That's an Audemar, Swayzee.

Oh this is what them fools be rapping about. Yep this baby cost about $72 thousand! For what, just to tell the time, get the fuck out of here with that, you're kidding! Nope! Well I know we can sell that then. Yeah this won't be a problem Sway; it's those damn paintings I'm worried about! Who do we know in the Art business? I don't have any idea

Skeet but they will look good on the wall.

Swayzee you fool nigga, these damn paintings cost more than our damn entire apartment building! Ha-ha! Show you right, show you right Skeet but hey, it is what it is. So let's get the hell out of here, I don't think it's much more. Hold on Sway I need a drink, let me see what's in the fridge. Man just look in that deep freezer over there, I'm sure ol boy got some beers in that thing. Damn I aint even see that! Yeah grab me one too! Alright Swayzee!

Skeeta makes his way over to the deep freezer that sits just before the steps leading into the Mansion. Hurry up

Skeet, so we can hit Onyx, I need some strippers in my life shawty. Bruh them ho's gone be there, give me a second, let me see what's in this freezer. Oh shit, look at this Motherfucker! What's wrong Skeet! Man you aint gone believe this; get your ass over here and look, you got to see it bruh! Bam! Sway slams the Rover door then heads over to the freezer with Skeet.

Well I'll be damn! Is that what I think it is Skeet! Yep! As the both of them stare down into the deep freezer, the garage light glimmers off several; sky blue and silver, plastic wrappers that contain 12 pure white keys of coke. Now this is what I'm talking about my nigga; Skeeta you believe this! I see it boy! Sway bends down, picks up three keys then heads to the truck. Come on shawty start loading this shit. I'm right behind you Sway! Man you got to be fucking kidding me! What is it now Skeeta? Skeet drops the keys back in the freezer; reaches in and comes up with two big shrink wrapped bundles of cash.

Bruh is that cash? Yeah man! Swayzee hastily runs back over to the freezer and picks up another bundle, looks at Skeeta then just laugh at what had just happened. Now, we can go to Onyx Swayzee! Ha-ha! Let's go trick off nigga, my treat! Ha-ha! Oh now your ass wanna treat, you too funny Swayzee!

4. Pros and Cons

Damn Tah; where's your food bitch? What! I said; where's your food girl; this damn fridge is empty. Kodi you know I don't cook! Well hurry your ass up and get dress so we can grab something to eat before you go on this date. I'm coming, hold your horses ho! You must really like this trick or something! Why you say that? Because you're getting dressed like yall going to a black and white ball or something!

Girl I have to stay top notch around this one; he's that Doctor I told you about. Ohhhhh yeah, this is the one you like; huh ho? Ummm, a little! Tah be careful girl; I warned you about falling for these tricks. Is he married? No he isn't! Well, that's beside the point, he's a trick and you're a ho! Man, miss me with that shit Kodi; I'm ready; come on let's go!

Umm-umm, look at you; this trick has you wearing the red bottoms. Girl he paid for them, so I could wear them, just for him! Now let's go; he's over off Dunwoody. Tahiry grabs her red DB bag, zips the top of her black fitted dress down just center of her cleavage, stops then looks at herself in the mirror on her living room wall, lifts her right foot, checks her red bottoms, smiles and heads for the door. Ok Ko, let's go; time to fuck this nigga to sleep.

Tahiry you're my bitch but you a fool! Girl I know you love me, here are the keys; you're driving! Ugh; who died and made you boss, bitch? Kodi, I still need to finish my make up! Alright Tah, you lucky you my girl! The ladies lock the apartment door, make their way to the black charger then head off to the I-285 bypass in route to Dunwoody.

I think I'm falling for this guy, for real Ko. So you really think that you can go from a whore to a house wife? I aint no whore Kodi, I'm just surviving girl. Remember you're the one that school me to this game. Yeah but you're getting it twisted, especially if you think this trick is going to take you seriously. He's paying you to leave him alone and not call him. Your job is to go and fuck him anytime he calls, not catch feelings bitch. But he's single, successful, got a banging ass townhouse and two Bentley's. I can see myself now, driving one of them fuckers to the Velvet Room. Ha-ha! Girl you just don't believe that fire is hot until it burns your ass. I'm a Boss Bitch Kodi; I got this, just watch.

Yeah ok, just be careful. Baby you already know, oh slow down you're turning right here into this community. Dammmnnn these are fly as fuck! I told you girl! Stop at the gate then press pound 334. Damn he gave you the access code. Yep, this pussy got him where he needs to be. Umm, so do you want me to wait for you or come in?

Nah, wait your ass out here; I'll be back in an hour. Well, I'm going across the street to grab a bite, my ass is hungry. Ok let me out, see you 59 minutes. Alright Ko, be careful! Tah steps out of the charger, checks her dress then makes her way up the cream colored brick stairway.

Ding-Dong! The big oak door swings open. Hello you must be Tahiry! Yeah that's me; who the hell are you and where's Doc? Oh he's in the kitchen we were waiting on you. I'm Jackie by the way. Well you still didn't tell me who you are, Jackie! Me; I'm a working girl just like you honey. Doc wanted a threesome today, so here we are! Move ho; fuck that! Doc! Doc! Where the hell are you! What's this shit! You didn't say anything about a threesome! I'm right here in the kitchen Tah and calm down, it's my money. Now bring your fine ass in here and give me a kiss. Nigga you got me twisted; I'm not fucking with a bitch that I don't even know.

Hold on trick, I'm not gone be; too many more bitches! Tah stops walking, looks back then swings her red purse at Jackie's face. Bap! Oh my God, you hit me! Bap-Bap! Tah swings again and again as Jackie tries to duck the plunging bag but gets bashed in her face.

Doc in his 5'6" stature runs from the kitchen and into the living room attempting to stop the brawl. Loud snaps ring in the air from the burning bag of popcorn in the microwave that began to pollute the air. Doc with all his might grab hold of Tahiry's arm as she continues to swing at Jackie's head. Wearing nothing but his polo robe and socks he slides left than right as the girls fast moving arms knock over his Tiffanies Chandelier lights. Bling! God dammit, both of you ratchet ho's! RIGHT NOW; GET THE FUCK OUT! NOW, I MEAN IT; GET THE FUCK OUT!

Why do I have to leave Doc; it was that slutty ass ho you invited over here! She aint nothing but a nasty, crack head bitch! Who you calling a crack head; ho!

You, Jack, Jill, whatever your damn name is! Tahiry shut your damn mouth; I'm disappointed with you! What has Jackie done to you, to cause you to act like a damn fool! Man if you have to ask; fuck you! I should knock your ass in the head with this bag too! You know what Tah; you're crazy, just leave my place.

Fine I was leaving anyway; I hope you and that crack head tranny have some fun! Bitch I'm more woman than your mother will ever be! What did you say about my momma- Pow! Oh shit, calm down Doc! Put the gun down! Tah get the hell out, next time I won't miss. I'm going nigga damn! I can't believe you pulled a gun out! Oh you don't think that I will put a cap in your pretty ass! Tahiry throws her bag over her shoulder, kneels down to dust the glass off her red bottoms, stands up then exits the Townhouse. Doc you can lose my number too punk, you're never taste this pussy again! Bam! He slams the door behind her as she walks out.

Man that bitch was crazy, was she your woman or something? No Jackie; just another call girl. No Doc that ho had feelings! Ring-Ring! Hello! Bitch where you at? About to eat my shrimp fried rice and wings; don't tell me that you're done already! Yeah, so bring your greedy ass on and pick me up! Damn Tah; let me get a to go box, I'll be there in a minute. Yeah ok; I'll be waiting outside the gate. Ok I'm coming.

Beep-Beep! Guys passing by Tah standing in front of the community gate, constantly beep their horns at her as they drive by, appalled by her stunning beauty and fitted dress. Effortlessly she ignores them as Kodi pulls up in the Charger. Girl what took you so long? Tah it was only 5 minutes since I talked to you, stop tripping. I aint tripping; that punk ass trick in there tripping! What do you mean Tah, do we need to go cap a fool? No I'm good Kodi, let's just go!

Alright just checking girl! I know but I really don't want to speak on it. Well I need to stop by Lennox Mall, you down? Yeah; what you going to get? Some new TRU Religion's. Umm, I need some too, you treating? I got you girl! What, you do! Shit let's hurry up before you change your mine! Ha-ha! Don't go there ho!

I'm just playing Ko. I know girl, I wanna hear some Tip you got some in here? You already know Kodi, just play disc 5; I got that shit programmed to my favorite track. Oh yeah; which one is that? 24's! Oh Kay that's that fire! Yep turn that thang up, drop all the windows and blast this thang while we're cruising down Peachtree. Ha-ha! Tahiry you a thug Bitch! Nah baby just a shawty from Decatur! Ha-ha! Girl stop!

"Money, hoes, cars and clothes, that's how all my niggaz roll." "Blowing dro on 24's" "That's how all my niggaz roll." Now in Buckhead, Atlanta; Kodi cruises in and out of traffic as they travel to Lennox square down busy Peachtree Street. Cars and Clothes, Fat bank rolls, that's how these two bitches roll! Oh shit, sing that thing Tah! That's how these two bitches roll! Yeah you aint know I had flows; did you Ko!

Alright now, let's not get ahead of ourselves Miss Tahiry. Don't hate Kodi, I got flow. Yeah ok; you wanna valet or park? Girl; go through valet! I aint trying to find no park at busy as Lennox! Hello ladies, welcome to

Lennox; enjoy your stay. Thank you baby; don't scratch my Charger. Oh no Ma'am; we will take good care of it. Thank you baby; come on Kodi give him the keys and let's go spend your money. Aint no worries Tah; you treating next trip! You know I got you girl. On the real though Tahiry, we might pick up a few tricks in here.

Kodi as long as their paying, I will serve their ass. That's what I'm talking about Tah, get money! Smack! Ouch ho! Why you smack my ass so hard. You know you like that Tah! Ko I aint fucking your ass, so stop trying. We'll see about that when the money is right. Now in that case I will be fucking the money not you. Ha-ha! Tahiry you stoopid! Ha-ha! I know! Oh girl; there's the TRU Religion Store, right there!

Kodi grabs Tah by the right arm and lead her into the store. Hello girls, welcome to TRU Religion; what can I get for you today? Hey baby; I need a size 5, low cut, so I can show off these hips and juicy ass! Ohhh kay Ma'am, we can make that happen. Ha-ha! Kodi your ass is crazy! What girl, I didn't pay for this body to hide it! Yeah I see! And will you be getting something Ma'am? Yeah let me look around some more first. Sure take your time and Ma'am I'll be back with your low cut, size fives. Thank you baby!

Damn! What Kodi? Did you see them two niggas walking by! No I didn't. You need to keep your eyes open for some tricks; we can at least get some drinks or food from somebody in this bitch. Kodi that's like taking candy from a baby, we'll take care of that after we're done here. Ok Miss Tahiry; I hear you superstar. Humph, you better know it! Ha-ha! You a mess Tah!

Ok Ma'am here's your size 5! Thanks baby, where's your fitting room? Oh I'm sorry, it's right there in the corner by the hats. Alright I'm going to try these on, make sure you take care of my girl, everything is on me! Yes Ma'am! I'll be back in a minute Tah! Take your time Kodi, I'm still deciding. Girl don't take all day, I want to eat too! Kodi take your ass in there and try on those jeans; I'll be ready. Tah you aint my Momma! Ha-ha! Nah that's Josephine; I can call her if you want me to! Ho shut up; I'll be back.

Did you see anything you like Ma'am? Um-hmm, I want to try on that jacket and shorts with the studs. Sure what size did you want; you look like a 4 or a maybe a 6. Aww you're so sweet, let me try a 6 honey. Ok I'll get that for you, be back in a sec. Thanks, you're such a gentleman! You're welcome; I'm just doing my job Ma'am. Honey call me Tahiry; I aint that old! Oh I'm sorry! It's ok! Tah! Hey Tah! What girl! What do you think! Damn, look at that ass in dem jeans gurl! It looks good don't it? Yeah you killing it Ko!

Ring-Ring! Ring-Ring! Tah is that your phone? Yeah but I can't find it! It's sitting on the jean rack. Where! Right there! Oh shit! Ring-Ring! Hello! Hi this is a collect call from the Dekalb County Jail, from inmate; "Meshaw!" to accept press number 1; to decline press number 2! Tah holds the phone away from her ear then looks down at it. Oh hell nah; no this nigga didn't! What's wrong Tah? This is Meesh calling me collect from the county. Beep! What did he say girl? Nothing, I just declined his ass! Girl you stupid!

Tahiry

Alright Miss Tah here's your size 6; do
you need to try them on? Yeah I better;
I'll be back, Kodi. Go ahead girl; I'll be
waiting at the counter after I put my
clothes back on. Excuse me bruh! Yes sir
how can I help you? When is the new
shipment coming in; I'm waiting on
them black sneakers. That will be
tomorrow sir; we can give you a call
when they come in if you want.

Nah that's alright shawty; I'll be back
tomorrow. Ummm-Ummm, didn't you
see him talking to me! My bad shawty
no disrespect, I'm about to head to the
bar, you want a drink or something?
Sure but I have to wait on my girl.
That's what's up is she fine as you?

Of course! Well where is she; let's ride! She's coming and my name is Kodi by the way. Nice to meet you Kodi, I'm Shaq! Ok girl we can go, they fit fine and who is this? Shaq this is my girl Tahiry. Tahiry this Shaq! Hey Shaq! Hi Tahiry, nice to meet you! Um-hmm. Hey baby; go ahead and ring these up for me. Sure no problem, will there be anything else? Nah that's it!

Hey Kodi; you guys can meet me downstairs at the bar over at the Hilton next door. Wait a minute, did I miss something Ko? Oh he's buying us some drinks girl. Oh really! Yes really! Alright calm down bitch, I heard you! When you guys get done, just meet over there, here's my number Kodi, put it in your phone. Alright Shaq, what is it? 404-989-7788! Got it! Cool, see yall in a bit shawty!

Kodi who in the hell was that 7 foot tall motherfucker! Another trick but he doesn't know it yet. Ko your ass is fool, that man don't need to buy no pussy. Nah hoe, he's gone buy a threesome, we're about to turn his tall ass out. Girl what the hell ever! Ma'am your total is $786.89! Thanks baby, charge this card. So how do you plan on setting this threesome up? Tah look in the mirror, what man can resist these two fine ass chicas. Nobody ho! Damn right!

Here are your bags ladies; thank you and come again! You're welcome! Now let's go get this paper Tah! Ring-Ring! Ring-Ring! Hold on Ko! Hello! This is a collect call from; "Meesh!" an inmate in Dekalb County Jail to accept press 1 to deny press 2. Beep! Hey baby; how you been girl? Meesh; why are you calling me, I told you I'm not fucking with your punk ass no more. I know Tah, I just need some money on my books, a nigga is living like a savage in here. Meshaw kiss my ass; eat that food they serve you. Don't you get three hot's and a cot! Click! Ooooh Tah; did you hang up on him! Hell yes I did!

Girl you too much! He'll be ok Kodi, besides I'm not his woman anymore no way! I hear that baby; we're here, time to get our drink on. Let's do it then, I sure hope that nigga got a check. Kodi and Tahiry step off the escalator; make their way over the cream ceramic tiles of Lennox mall then enter the Hilton hotel side entrance just as a patron exits.

Girl that man aint even here! Didn't he give you his phone number Kodi? Oh yeah; let me see where he's at! Ring-Ring! Ring-Ring! Ring-Ring! This trick aint even answering the phone! Ring-Ring! Ring-Ring! Hello; thank you for calling Lucky Wing! What your order! Oh hell no! Kodi takes the phone from her ear then looks at the number. What's wrong Ko! This fool gave me the number to a Chinese restaurant! Ha-ha! Say word bitch! Man that shit aint funny! Girl; come on and let's go! Ha-ha! You got played Kodi! Shut up Tah!

Ok, you two bitches sit down right here and wait for a pimp. I'll be right back with some grub for you ho's! Don't be looking at no niggas either; or I'll smack the fuck out of yall asses! You hear me! The two new recruits sit there in silence as Tiger continues to rant and rave. I said did you hear me! Yeah we heard you. No bitch, you need to say; Yes Daddy we hear you! Ok daddy! Bap! Ouch! No ho; say it! Just like I said! Ok I'm sorry; Yes Daddy we hear you! Better, now sit there and be quiet.

Hi sir; welcome to the Decatur Deli; how can I help you? Hey my man; let me get two cheese burgers with some onion rings and two of them Ice Tea's. Sure, will there be anything else sir? Yeah that's for my ho's; let me get one of those Philly cheese steaks with a coke. Alright I have two cheese burgers with a side of onion rings- That's two onion rings right there shawty! Oh I'm sorry; two orders of onion rings, two ice teas and a Philly with a coke! Yep how much is that?

Your total is $15.73 sir! Damn how about I get one of my bitches to give you some head and we call it even. Ha-ha! I'm serious shawty; see those two ho's right there, take your pick! Sir I wish I could! Shawty ask your manager can you go to the bathroom and I'll send her in with you to suck you off. Come on shawty, I know you aint gone turn those fine ho's down! Alright man, hold on a minute; let me get somebody to cover me. Now that's what I'm talking about pimpin, go ahead and throw in another cheeseburger for the road too! Ha-ha! Alright Sir; I got you! Cool shawty; I'll be at the table with my bitches.

Ok lil bitch; my man at the cash register just paid for a blow job. So when he goes in the bathroom; I want you to take your yellow ass in there and serve him good. You got that! Yeah I got it. Excuse me! Yes daddy; I got it. That's better.

The two nervous women could only sit there and wonder about what really happened at that counter. Fear travel through their adolescent minds as Tiger mentally controlled their every move. New to ATL they had no idea how real the streets were and how easy they could get caught up. The look in their paranoid eyes told the true story and how they regret now leaving Minnesota.

Hey bitch! Bitch! Huh; daddy! He's ready; now go in there and make me proud! Yes daddy! And you; stay your pretty mocha ass right here; I'm going to gets this grub, a pimp hungrier than a motherfucker! Ok daddy.

Etched names splatter the ceramic wall tiles and mirror alike in the tainted men's bathroom. The disgusting smell of stale urine, penetrates the misty air as the cashier walks into the stall to wait for the sexy young red bone.

Ok pervert, drop your pants and don't nut in my mouth either. Damn girl, what's the point? Hey nigga; do you want your dick sucked or not! Ok come on; I only have 10 minutes. The cashier grabs the short sexy red bone by the head as he sat calmly on the toilet seat while she went down on him. Her pretty head bobbed up and down as he watched her in action. Damn baby your mouth feels good! Ummm, you like that nigga! Hell yeah! Slurp-slurp! Slurp-

slurp! Oh lord; slow down baby; I'm not ready to cum yet! Slurp-slurp! Slurp-slurp! The cashier arched back on the toilet seat as she sucked harder and harder. Bam-Bam! What the fuck, who is it! Bam-Bam! Alright Bitch; time is up! Hold on girl where are you going? That's it baby; daddy said your time is up! Bam-Bam! Let's go! Coming daddy!

Sorry hun! Come on man, I didn't even finish. That aint my fault shawty; how much head did you think a cheeseburger was gone get you! A CHEESBURGER! Bitch shut up and take your ass up front, can't you see two men talking! Yes daddy! As I was saying shawty; if you want more it's gone cost you! How much? $50 playa! $50! Yes sir!

Man you aint right! Hey; aint no love lost shawty; it's just business. Man that's fucked up! Life aint fair young buck, you better be getting back to work, I think your boss was looking for you.

Meanwhile, over in Lithonia, Flawless visits one of her regulars for an early session. Damn Flawless; your pussy is wet as I don't know what girl! Dude you only have 15 minutes left, are you going to sit there and rub my pussy all night, put on that condom and fuck me already. Alright Flaw; be patient, what's the rush? I was only trying to help your ass out but it's your money do what you want. The trick stands to his feet, slides on the rubber then pulls Flawless to the edge of the bed, her legs up in the air.

Ummm, now that's what I'm talking about, fuck this pussy boy! So, Flawless this is like my 4th time seeing you; how come you never call me or anything? Umm, just be quiet and keep stroking. I'm serious Flawless! Umm-umm! Ugh nigga damn, fuck me! Answer me Flawless? Man this is business, why are you trying to make it all personal and shit? Because I like you! Umm, you need to stop tripping dude. You pay me, to not call you; this is supposed to be stress free pussy!

Flawless pauses at the hint of compassion in his voice, looks up at him then pushes him off. Back up man, let me turn over, I want you to hit it from the back. See, you're not taking me seriously! I'm listening, put it in already, we're running out of time. The huge King size bed, bounce and squeak as he stroke her from behind. So what's up then? Man don't you have a wife, what will she have to say about that! Nah I don't, ummm this thing wet girl. Dude stop lying, you're fucking me in yalls bed right now. Just keep paying me for this pussy and stop catching feelings.

Oh, so you don't feel the same way Flawless? I mean you're cool but this is just business, I love fucking you though. YOU BROKE DICK MOTHER FUCKER! Shit; when did you get here! Man who the hell is this! BITCH I'M HIS NIGGA; GET YOUR STINKING FISH ASS OUT!

NOW BITCH! Darrel I can't believe you're cheating on me! Flawless jumps up from the bed, grabs the cash off the dresser, stops then look at the two men arguing. Hell nah, nigga you're gay? Wow aint this some shit! LEAVE BITCH! I'm going, I'm going, umm-umm, aint this a trip!

Ring-Ring! Yeah Flaw, what's up? I'm ready Skeet, come scoop me! I'm about to turn in now, that was fast, everything cool? Man yall aint gone believe this; where's my girl at? She's right here beside me Flawless. Ok I'm walking up the sidewalk, is that you coming towards me now? Yep; I see you. What's wrong Skeet? Nothing Stallion; she said she was good. Umm, I bet something crazy happened. Skeet comes to a complete stop, unlocks the Range doors then Flawless jumps in the back seat.

Damn it smells good in this bitch, let me hit that loud! Here girl, now what the hell happened, you're just shaking your head. Alright Stallion, so me and the nigga getting our fuck on then all of a sudden this deep voice yells out! "DARREL I KNOW YOU AINT CHEATIN ON ME!" Stop lying girl! I aint lying Stallion; that boy gay and his boyfriend lives with him! See that's that down low shit, a bitch got to be careful out here with these trifling ass niggas. Damn that's fucked up right there baby girl! I sure hope you made that fool scrap up? Come on Skeet; I aint no fool now. Alright I was just making sure.

Man I need another blunt; that just blew my mind yall. I'll roll another one Flaw you can finish that. Thanks girl, I appreciate it! I'm hungry; you guys want something to eat? Hell yeah Skeet; are you treating? Yep I'm about to pull into Wendy's; which combo you want? Aww nigga; we aint too proud, get me a chicken combo, Stallion tell him what you want! Get me that Bacon cheeseburger! Ha-ha! See yall just got the munchies from hitting that loud but I got it though! Thanks baby! It's all good ladies! "Welcome to Wendy's; can I take your order please?"

****

Damn it's hot out here today Tah! Hell yeah it is, so hurry your ass up Swayzee! I won't be long; I just need to get some money out of my savings account, my damn baby momma tripping about this child support. Stop playing Sway; I didn't even know you had a kid. Yeah, that bitch rarely lets me see him though. See that's crazy right there man. Yeah I know; I'll be back in a few, keep the AC going. Shit; you think I aint! Ha-ha. Tah you crazy!

Tahiry leans back in the driver seat as Sway steps out of the Charger and walks into Atlanta Bank & Trust. 108 degree heat, force sweat beads to form on his forehead as he adjusts his belt to tighten his baggy jeans. Sway pulls his all black ATL fitted cap down over his sweaty forehead, straightens his Polo button up then stands in line behind the other patrons.

Hey! Hey! Hey Swayzee! Hey Tahiry, I thought you were going to wait in the car. Man it's too hot, I just got my hair done too. Nah I'm going over there to chill in the A.C. Ok I won't be long, just give me a few minutes. Yeah take your time, I'm in no hurry. Next in line please! As the teller calls for Swayzee, Tah takes a seat in the waiting area to enjoy the ice cold air blowing down from the vent above not like in her car when the sunlight beaming through her car window still managed to eject heat.

Hey; I need to take out some money!
Sure I can help you with that Sir! Can I
have your I.d and Bankcard please? Oh
my bad baby; I should have had it out
already.

Swayzee reaches behind his back to
retrieve his wallet as she looks on. With
his left pointer finger over his lips, he
signals for the teller to be quiet. Shhh!
Her smile quickly turns to a frown, eyes
wide as golf balls and her hands starts
shaking nervously as he places his piece
on the counter then in a low voice he
whispers. You know what this is; give
me $15,000.00 right now; don't scream
or I will blast's your pretty ass. You got
that?

She shakes her head to agree. Good, now put the money in this bag. Sway reaches in his jeans and pulls out a folded black nylon gym bag, unrolls it then throws it on the counter. I don't have all day bitch, keep quiet and load it up. Silently she loads the bag as her fellow bankers tend to their customers, no matter how hard she prayed to herself for them to look. Come on ho, that's enough, now zip it up. Swayzee pulls the bag off the counter, tucks his 357 in the front of his jeans then hastily leaves the stressed teller there in awe.

The loud screeching sound from his sneakers running across the polished tile floor catches Tahiry's attention. Tah come on; let's go! Hold on Sway; what the Hell! Girl let's go! Confused, she runs out behind him, jumps in the car, starts it then pulls off.

Nigga tell me you just didn't do what I think you did! Tah, just drive the damn car; get the fuck out of here! Sway you aint about shit, why do you always have to put me in the middle of something! You know you like this gangster life shawty, now turn in that parking garage right there, at Atlantic Station. Nigga you're going to get me locked up, I know it! Shaking her head in disbelief, she takes a quick right into Atlantic station, drives to the back then pulls into the parking garage.

I know half of that is mine, right! Bitch you crazy; I'll buy you a steak! Boy I'll bust you in your mouth with this stiletto, don't play me! Ha-ha! I'm just playing Tah, you can have these two stacks. Mannnn, two thousand dollars, this can only get me one pair of red bottoms. Shawty you crazy; come on let's go grab something to eat, we can go shopping after. Now you're talking Sway! You know I got you baby; I was just fucking with you about that steak. Oh I'm still down for that too! Ha-ha! Damn Tah!

Loud sounds of police sirens sound in the background seem to get closer and closer to them by the second. Alright Tah hurry your ass up, let's start walking to the restaurant before they roll up on us. I'm ready but you need to throw that button up in the trash or something. Damn, good thinking shawty, help me take it off. Tahiry sits her purse on the lot then pulls off Sway's shirt from behind after he unbuttons it then places it in her purse. Alright now we're ready. Swayzee turns his ATL fitted to the back as they head towards the garage exit then to Atlantic station.

Damn Sway, I think it's too late, those sirens are getting closer. Are you sure that you didn't get caught? Tah it was a smash and grab baby, fuck it! So what are you saying? I'm saying I don't know; I'm sure they got camera's shawty! Man you need to be sharper than that, let's go into this theater; we can lay low for a few hours. Good idea Tahiry; I want to see that Rise of the Planet of the Apes anyway! Alright come on, did you bring some cash?

Yep, I got a stack- Hello, welcome to Atlantic Station, Stadium 16 theaters; which movie did you guys want to see? Hey baby, can we get two for the Planet of Apes? Yes Ma'am; that will be $18.50! Sway; pay the lady! Oh here you go shawty! Thank you Sir! Swayzee and Tahiry make their way into the cool air conditioned building away from the heat and most of all, the police.

Swayzee please give me a heads up the next time you plan on doing something stupid. Shawty I told you I needed to get some cash to pay my child support! Nigga you didn't say that you were going to use a damn gun either!

Ring-Ring! Ring-Ring! Hold on let me get this, it's Skeeta! Hey bruh; what's up! Man where is your ass at? At the movies with Tah! Which one? Atlantic station, why? Shawty; yall's ass is all over the news they have your face on camera and Tahiry's Charger! Shit; for real! Yep; we need to get out of town, me and Kodi are coming to pick yall up, stay right there! Where we going Skeet! Charlotte bruh! Alright; for show!

What he talking about Sway? Tah we need to leave town, they have my face on the news and they know what kind of car I left in. What! So they got my fucking car on the news? Yep! Man I'm not messing with your ass no more, I swear! Come on shawty, this is the life of a G! Sway, kiss my ass!

5. Queen City

Tahiry hurry your ass up, just pack your feminine needs, we can go shopping for clothes when we get to the QC. Kodi, I'm taking more than that bitch! Girl, just make it quick; Sway and Skeeta are out front already waiting on us. Alright just three minutes Ko! Oh shit bitch! What Kodi! The news! What about it? Look, it's you and Swayzee! Tahiry runs up front to see what was going on.

"Good evening Atlanta; here's some Breaking News from Channel 8 live at 6!" "Local Authorities are on the look-out for these two individuals." "The

woman pictured at the bottom of the
screen is wanted for questioning about a
Bank Robbery that took place in Atlanta
earlier today." "A car registered to her
was used to get away from the crime
scene." "The young woman goes by
Tahiry, police have not released the last
name of the lady as of yet."

"The photo that you see here was giving
to us by our research team and was
pulled from the Department of Driver
Service's public records." "The picture
we are showing now is of the man
wanted for the robbery, as you can see
here; he has on a black ATL ball cap
pulled down over his eyes." "There are
no leads on who the man is at this
time."

"If you recognize any one of these individual's, please call the Fulton County Police Department or your local Authorities, your name will not be released for giving out this information." "This has been your local news at 6; we will be right back after these messages."

Oh my God, did you just see that! Yes Tah, I did, now let's go! Hastily she runs and drops anything that she could grab into her overnight bag while cursing out loud because of the situation that Sway had gotten her in. Dammit, I knew I shouldn't have driven that boy nowhere, now look at this shit! Ring-Ring! Ring-Ring! Ring-Ring! Tah it's your phone! Ring-Ring! Ring-Ring! Look at the caller I.d, what does it say! Ring-Ring! It's your Mom! Damn, I'll call her back! Ring-Ring! Ring-Ring! Ring-Ring! She's still calling Tah! Fuck! Ok take my bag to the car; I'm coming; let me talk to her! Alright girl, hurry up!

Ring-Ring! Hello! Tahiry! Yes Mom! What in the hell! I didn't do it mom! Well; why do they have your picture all on the news then child! I gave my friend a ride to the bank; I didn't know that jack ass was going to rob it! Baby you need to call them and let them know that! Yeah right; they're not going to believe me! Tahiry if you don't, I will! Mom I will take care of it! When child! Later! Later; what the hell do you mean by later! I'm calling the cops right now and I'm on the way to your house, stay right there until get there! Mom no! Click! Shit, she hung up! Beep-Beep! Beep-Beep! Swayzee blows the horn for her to hurry just as she steps out of the door, locks it and runs as fast as she can to the Rover.

Kodi pushes the back passenger door open as Tah approaches. What took you so long Tah; you know the cops are looking for us. Bap! Bap! Bap! Oh shit, stop Tah; that hurt God dammit! Bap! Girl would you stop hitting me with your phone! Fuck you Sway! Bap! Ouch! Skeeta just drive off man, let's get out of GA! Bap! Bap! Look at what you got me into Swayzee, nigga if they come for me, I'm giving your bitch ass up!

Tah it's going to be cool; we're just gone kick it in Charlotte for a few days and let everything die down, then you can call them when you get back and tell them that your car got stolen while you were out of town. Man my car is still where we left it! It won't be when we get back, I've already made some calls! Bap! Ugh! You make me sick Sway! Ouch, just chill shawty, stop hitting me with that damn phone!

Skeeta makes his way several miles up South Hairston and pulls off Jimmy Carter blvd. then onto the I-85 N interchange. We will be there in a few hours yall then we can kick it. I know you owe me a new car too, punk! I got you Tah, I got you! Girl I need to smoke, roll up some of that loud. I already got one ready Tah! Thanks Kodi!

Skeeta, slow your ass down! Be quiet and let me drive Kodi! I'm just saying fool; you know there's a target on our backs and you going 25 miles over the damn speed limit! Fuck the damn police; they can't catch me anyway. Ko, them fools got a death wish, that's why we're in this mess now. Tahiry I don't know why you're acting like you're so damn special, you aint no better than me! Sway; I think when I do something; you don't; that's the difference between me and you.

Yeah whatever; let's see you plan something the next time then; all I know is we're on the way to Charlotte to have a good time and we got 15 stacks to blow! See, that's what I'm talking about; do yall hear this fool! He aint got a damn clue; Sway just stop talking to me! Kiss my ass Tah! Yeah you wish!

Man, both of you need to shut up; it's too late to be crying about it now! Let's just chill and think this thing through; I aint trying to stay in Charlotte forever! I hear you Skeet but your boy has some serious issues. Sway smirks and ignores the conversation as Skeet accelerates the Rover through traffic and speeds up I-85. Look at him Skeet; he thinks this shit is funny. Hey just calm down Tah; it will all work out baby. Man that's what your mouth say! Skeet; fuck her shawty turn up the damn radio; I don't need to hear this crap! After few hundred miles and minutes of uncomfortable silence later they find themselves only 30 miles outside of the Queen City, they could see the Skyline on the Horizon as Sway adjust the radio station. "What's up people; this is your boy Danny D." "Don't forget I will be spinning at the Bobcats-Lakers game tonight; so come out and support the Home team!" "Next up we got that new cut from that boy Future; Tony Montana!"

Hey Skeet; we're hungry can you stop so we can eat, I need to get away from

Sway's punk ass. Yo shawty; you can chill with that attitude, what's done is done, you still my folk no matter what. I know I fucked up but I'm gone fix it Tah, it aint no thing. Umm-hmm, whatever Swayzee! Skeet pulls off the interstate, veers onto Brookshire blvd. then heads uptown Charlotte.

Yo Skeet hit that one joint we went to last time we came through! Which one Sway? That strip joint! Man we don't want to see no ass; we want food! Chill Tah; this place has some good food though. Alright I don't care; let's just go. Oh yeah Skeet, it's the Uptown Cabaret! Yeah ok, I remember, they had that good ass buffet! Yep! Cool it's just around the corner from the stadium.

Yeah let's stop there first Skeet then we can head up the block and get a suite at the Westin. Sounds like a plan to me Skeeta; are you going to visit your little brother while we're here? Umm-hmm; I'll call him later. I didn't know you had family here Skeeta! Oh it's my half-brother; one of my pops many kids.

Damn this place is packed; aint no damn parks! Just park across the street behind that laundry matt shawty; we'll be good. I sure hope the food is good! It's straight Tah; at least it was the last time I came here. Ok Skeeta; if it's not, you're buying me room service! I got you baby! Sway, Kodi, Tahiry and Skeet all get out of the Rover, walk across the street and enter the busy building on the corner of Morehead and South Tryon.

Ring-Ring! Hold on yall, my phone is ringing! Ring-Ring! Hello, this Skeeta; who this? Hey big bro, what's good? What up Slim, we just got to Charlotte! Oh yeah, why you aint call me man? I was going to lil bro, how you been? Hey Skeet, we'll be inside, we're hungry! Alright yall, I'll be in, in a minute. So Slim; what's good, how's school? It's straight but I was calling because I just seen a picture of your boy Sway on the news robbing a bank. Are you still hanging with that nigga!

Yeah he's here with me now! Damn Skeet; be careful, the cops are looking for him and some bitch. I know lil bro, she's here too. Bruh you're just asking for trouble, where are yall staying? We're about to get a room at the Westin after we finish eating. That's what's up, call me after and I'll come through.

Alright Slim, are you going to catch the bus uptown? Nah bro; I got my license! Damn lil bruh, moving up! Cool, I'll hit you later than. Sweet, later Skeet! Later Slim.

Hot macaroni and cheese, fried chicken, filet mignon, mashed potatoes and greens scent up the Gentlemen's club as patrons sit at their tables enjoying the daily buffet. Swayzee, Kodi and Tahiry join the others in line to fix their plates while half naked ladies converse with patron's through-out the club. Now this is surprising, I've never seen a spread like this in a strip club, back in the A!

Trust me Tahiry, there's a few back home that can compare. How do you know Ko? Girl I'll take you when we get back; I can't tell all of my secrets. I hear you bitch! Hey yall need to be scoping out this crowd, I see some good marks in this piece. Nigga we're already on the run and you're still trying to get into more shit. Look Tah, it's ride or die baby, you can't be a part time criminal shawty. I aint no criminal Sway, you just always take it upon yourself to involve me in your mess. The way I see it, if you didn't want to be down, you would have left a long time ago. Nobody asked you to keep coming around. Dude whatever; Kodi get that fool before I throw my plate at him.

Look both of you guys just calm down, what's done is done. I'm going to sit down; you deal with her ass Kodi. Tahiry I know you're upset girl but it's a better way to handle this. Yeah I know how to handle it; I'm gone be in charge from now on. The problem is, aint no order to this little click we got. We fucking and sucking here and there. Skeeta got some random bitches on the team, that we know nothing about and Swayzee just do shit without thinking.

Oh so you can do better, Miss high post! I sure can Ko, watch me! Alright I'm gone do just that, and when Sway slaps your ass don't come crying to me! Girl I wish that fool would put his hands on me; he won't take another breath. Ummm! Aint you the gangster bitch all of a sudden. Ko somebody has to take over or we'll all be dead soon. Look at what we're doing; RUNNING!

Alright, alright, you have a point; I got your back, no matter what! I know you do girl, watch me work! Hey yall, where's Swayzee? Over there sitting down, aint you getting a plate Skeet? Yep; that was my lil brother, he's coming by the room later. Ok cool can't wait to meet him; we'll be over at the table with Swayzee. Kodi and Tahiry make their way through the crowded lunch hour crowd. Tables with white table clothes and lit candles accent the décor as topless dancers and incoming customers crowd the area where Swayzee's sitting.

So Sway, Tahiry has an idea. Yeah what kind of idea Ko? I'll let her tell you. Well, spit it out shawty! Look Sway, I know you and I have been bumping heads for a minute but I think I have a solution. Oh really! Yeah; are you gone hear me out? You got 5 minutes Tah! I think that you guys should let me organize everything. With a fried chicken leg in his right hand he looks over at Tahiry. What you mean by that shawty?

I'm saying that we need some structure; we can get more money that way. And how the fuck; are you gone organize something when you're the bitch that's always too scared. Tah hastily reaches under the table and pulls a piece from her bag. Click-Click! Hold up nigga, I aint never been scared of nothing, not even your stupid ass! What you doing girl, put that away! Shut up Kodi!

Umm-hmm; look at you now Sway. I'm a bad bitch though, aint I nigga. Shawty; take that gun away from my face now. Or what! Tah please put that thing up, we're in the club. Fuck this club; I'm gone be running shit and aint a damn thing you can do about it Swayzee! Skeet finally makes his way to the table and stumbles onto the current situation.

Tahiry if you don't put that thing in your purse! I'm good Skeet, just showing Sway who the Boss is! Man are you two going to ever quit it? Hell no, not until he says I'm the boss. She shakes the gun in his face. Go ahead; say it Sway! Tahiry put that thing away! See, now it's time to go, here's security! I don't care about no damn bouncer Skeet!

Ma'am please put the gun away and can you guys come with me? With a quick jerk; Tah pulls the gun away from Swayzee's face. Bap-Bap! Sway smacks Tah twice across the face. Ouch you motherfucker! Bitch, don't you ever put a gun in my face! It's cocked and ready for your ass Sway; hit me again! Ma'am! Sir! Let's go! Okay, ok, I'm coming! Sir that means you too! Hold on shawty; we're leaving, let me finish my chicken! Now Sir!

The bright daylight almost blinds them as they exit the strip club, still hungry and in no better position than they were before. Yo let's go to the hotel, check in then order room service. We have a few things to discuss anyway, because if I'm going to be rolling with you clowns it has to be some order with this shit. Shawty who do you think you're talking to? You Swayzee, especially! What's the problem, Kodi nor Skeeta, has anything to say about it!

Tahiry what do you know about the crime life? Not much but I got common sense and I'm quick on my feet, you guys can handle the dirty work, I'll just organize it, so that we won't get in any trouble; like we're in now. Yeah I hear you. Come on Sway; give my girl a chance; the way I see it; it can't hurt!

We'll see what happens Kodi. Bruh it can't hurt! Alright Tah; when we get to the room; let's draw up a game plan!

Ha-ha! Now you're making sense Sway; I knew you would come around; I might even give you some pussy now. Ha-ha! Bitch you crazy; that's why I love you! Kodi you already know girl! Ok get in the car, the hotel is just around the corner!

Ring-Ring! Ring-Ring! Hey Skeet; you drive shawty, I need to take this call. Ring-Ring! Yo what up pimp! Hey Swayzee; it's done! Thanks pimp; make sure it doesn't come up now! Oh it won't playa; we stripped that Charger good, hell we even sliced the frame too! Thanks pimp; I will hit you off when we get back to the A. For show Sway; see you when you get back! Alright shawty!

Swayzee jumps in the passenger seat as Skeet starts to back up. Hey Tah; we took care of that problem. What problem Sway? Your car! What about it? It's gone; no one can find it now! Cool-hold on, wait a minute! You need to get me a new car nigga! Calm down Tah; I got you covered; what kind of car you want? A Benz! Damn girl; you didn't hesitate! Ha-ha! Come on Kodi; you know what it is girlfriend! Already baby!

Well! Well what Tah! Don't act like you didn't hear me! I heard you; Skeet, keep straight, we're not staying at the Westin. Drive a few more blocks up and stop at the Luxor Renaissance Hotel. Right there on 5th! Why are we going there

275

bruh? We need to get Tah a new car; they have a covered parking deck! True but so does the Westin! Yeah but more cars are at the Luxor and they don't have security gates that requires the room key. Oh that's smart right there Swayzee; let' do it!

Damn, your ass is too cheap to just go buy me a car Sway! I don't need all these problems, how in the fuck am I supposed to feel comfortable driving around in a stolen car? Tah chill, we can fix that! Yeah, you better tell me how before I drive any damn thing! Look shawty, my partner in College Park can switch the VIN numbers to match the car, it will be registered with insurance and all that shit. Alright; I hear you Mr. Swayzee!

 Hey yall, grab your bags, we're pulling up to the Hotel. Skeet forget about all that, just pull up to the valet baby, let them get the bags. I'm too tired after this long ride to be pulling some bags anyway! Good idea Kodi! Tah, you have to work smarter not harder, right! Yep; you tell him Ko! They can't know; huh! Apparently not! Ha-ha! As the cocaine white Range Rover cruises into the red brick drive way, several gentlemen, draped in blue blazers overlapping white tuxedo shirts wait curbside to assist oncoming motorist.

Tahiry

Hi folks; welcome to Luxurious Renaissance Suites! Are you guys checking in? Yeah man and we have some bags in the back too! No problem Sir; we will be happy to get those for you; go ahead and check in; leave me your keys and the bell hop will bring your bags up! Cool, thanks shawty; what's your name? I'm Daniel Sir! Nice to meet you D; I'm Skeeta, this is my nigga; Swayzee and those two bitches is Kodi and Tahiry! Bitches; I got your bitches Skeeta; keep acting up, you won't be getting any of this pussy later, I can promise you that!

Skeeta I aint even gone follow you up but you were wrong for that. Tah, Ko, you guys know I was just fucking with you. Kiss my ass Skeeta! Tah! Bye Skeeta, go with your boy and check us in, me and Ko are going to the bar! Girl them two fools are going to get us locked up or shot. Run this shit Tah! I'm about to, as soon as we get to that room; we're all going to have a sit down. Look at you, talking about a sit down; you think you a Boss already. Cause I am girl! Ha-ha! We'll see Tahiry!

Hello Gentlemen; welcome to Luxor Suites; did you guys have a reservation? No shawty; we need two suites. Pardon me? Oh don't mind him baby; it's just some ATL slang. He calls everyone shawty. But no we don't have a reservation, can we get two suites, next to each other. Sure we have a few available joining suites. Thanks, charge it to this debit card. Great, can I have your I.D as well? Sure!

So what do you think about what Tahiry said Skeeta? What, her running shit! Yeah! Man, I say let's see what kind of mind she has; it can't hurt. I'm gone give her two weeks shawty and that's it. She might just surprise us Sway! Yeah what the fuck ever, that bitch aint got no heart. Ha-ha! Bruh you crazy; wait it out. Two weeks shawty, two weeks! Alright guys, here are your two keys, rooms 902 and 904! Thanks baby!

No, hold up shawty, we're gone need two more keys; one for me and another for him too. Sure no problem, here you go! Thanks shawty! Skeeta where them ho's go? They went to the bar.

Skeeta and Swayzee walk away from the cherry oak counter then down the red and gold carpet hallway in route to the elevator. Skeet hit Kodi up on the cell and let her know which rooms we're in. You late nigga; I already texted her! Cool; I hope they have some good food; I can eat a whole cow! Bruh I don't care how it taste, this weed gone make it good anyway. You stupid Skeet!

Ladies I hope that you're enjoying your drinks! Yes baby, thank you, can you fix us another round? Sure Ma'am! Call me Tahiry baby! Sure Tahiry, coming right up! So are you going to give Sway some girl? Kodi let's talk about something else! Damn bitch, did you see that! What Ko! Girl, look out the window; turn around, do you see that black CL that just pulled up in front of the hotel.

Oh my God; I got to have it! Ha-ha! You better tell Swayzee to get you one! I don't need him; watch this! Tah come back, what are you doing! Soft white light from the gold chandelier above, cast shadows over the cream bar seat where Tah once sat. Her empty glass held melted ice cubes and shades of red lipstick mask the rim.

Quietly she makes her way out the entrance, past the guest then stands among the valet crew. She walks over to the Valet stand then sneaks one of the embroidered blue Valet jackets, slides it on then stands at the curb. The passenger side door of the Black, CLS 550 opens; Red bottom, Louis Vuitton's, softly touch the drive way, draped by a black sequence evening gown that lace a 5'10" hour glass figure. A 7 foot male exits the driver side then accompanies the elegant 5'10" hour glass model. Hello Ma'am, Sir; welcome to Luxor suites; would you like for me to park your car? Hell yeah, what kind of question is that?

I'm sorry Ma'am, I didn't know if you guys were here for Dinner or needed to park in the over-night lot. What's your name honey? Tahiry Ma'am! Well

Tahiry; is this your first day? Yes Ma'am! Ok that explains it! Baby, stop tripping and give her these keys, here; give them to her. Tahiry don't pay her no mind, she can be a bitch sometimes. Oh it's no problem Sir; which lot did you want it in, short or long stay? We're only coming for dinner, I'm sorry. It's no problem; I'll park it on the first level for you! Great; baby would you give her the keys already! Here! Thanks, you guys enjoy your dinner!

Tahiry looks over her shoulder at the couple entering the Hotel, makes her way to the driver side, starts the car then drives into the parking garage while dialing her cell. Ring-Ring! Ring-Ring! Tah, where are you? Bitch I'm driving that Benz! Tah stop lying! Kodi I'm serious as hell; go to the room and lay low; I'm about to call Swayzee and have him come drive this fucker back to Charlotte tonight! Tah you're a fool! No ho; I'm a boss!

Yeah you are! I'm going up to the room, hurry up and call him! Ok bye Ko! Ring-Ring! Ring-Ring! Hey shawty what's up! Meet me on the 5th level parking deck! For what Tah, I'm just about to order something to eat. Nigga that food has to wait! Shawty you tripping! Sway I just stole a Black CL 550; I'm driving it now; I need you to drive it back to the A tonight! What! Where did you get it and where is Kodi's ass?

She's on the way up to the room; I perpetrated like I was a Valet and they handed me the keys, they just went to dinner so you got about an hour or so to get the fuck out of town. Damn shawty; I'm coming; that was some trill shit though! No Nigga; Boss shit! Yeah you did that; I'm on the way to the garage now! Cool; see you in a sec Swayzee!

The loud CL 550 engine, echo off the cement garage walls as Tahiry accelerates at every turn in route to level 5. Swayzee waits anxiously in the shadows while the engine roars closer as she pulls in front of him. Damn shawty, this is clean as a motherfucker! Aint it though, Sway! Hell yeah, look at this cream leather, I wonder how much this thing cost Tah! A few stacks, I'm sure. I bet! So did you make the call yet, we're running out of time.

Oh we're good shawty; my man Spence out in College Park is going to chop it! No fool; don't chop it, I wanna keep it! Tah I've been doing this since 99 shawty. So I got this; don't worry yourself. You better! Because this pretty bitch is mine, change the VIN number or something. We can get that done too but it's going to cost more.

I don't care how much it cost Sway, you owe me! I know Tahiry just get out of the car, so I can head back to Atlanta. Spence is expecting me by 10 tonight.

Ok; call me when you get to College Park; I'll let Skeet and Kodi know what's up. Alright Tah! Errrrrrrr! Errrrrr! Tah stands there watching Sway as he spins off then down the ramp. She can still hear the engine roar the further Sway drives away from the 5th floor parking deck, her panties get a little wet at the sound of the tires screeching as it darts down the street.

Ring-Ring! Ring-Ring! This is Spence; what's poppin? Hey shawty; this Sway; I'm headed back to the A in a hot one! What you got boy! One of those, brand new CLS 550's! Brand new! Yep! Like 2011 new! Yes sir! What you trying to do with it Sway? Ol girl wants to keep it, so make it legit pimp. Nigga that's gone take at least 4 days before the clone VIN numbers come back. Well do what you got to do Spence. I'm about 3 hours away just left Charlotte good.

 Alright; what color is it and is it a V8 or 6? Black with cream interior and it's an 8! Straight my nigga; I'll order the VIN's from Mexico off line right now, just bring it straight to College Park so we can stash it until the VIN's come in. That's what it is shawty, see you in a few! You got it; holler at you later, Swayzee! The shiny, black Benz disappears in the distance as it jets in and out of traffic up interstate 85 South in route to the A.

Ring-Ring! Ring-Ring! Hello! What's up lil bro? Aint shit Skeet; you guys check in yet? Yeah but we're at the Luxurious suites instead. Ok I'm not far from there; I can be there in 30 minutes. Alright lil bro see you in a bit, we're going to order some room service and get cleaned up. Handle your business Skeet; see you later big bro!

Bitch that motherfucker road so good, honey it was like gliding on air! Tah you crazy; where is it now? Shit; Swayzee has it, he's driving back to Atlanta as we speak. Girl; stop playing! Kodi does it look like I'm playing. Umm-umm-umm! Damn Tah; what you do to my boy? What you mean Skeet? That fool just don't up and leave without telling somebody! Man he told me and now I'm telling yall, so what's the problem? Aint no problem Tah, just asking baby; you sure you aint give my boy none of that high post pussy of yours?

Skeet he never even smelled my pussy; and it's gone stay that way until he recognize that I'm the boss! What! You tell him Tah; he aint ready girl! He damn sure isn't Kodi; but I'll get him right. Looks like you already got him right to me Tah. That's my boy, like my damn brother and he aint never did no shit like this. Just leave without telling a brother. I'm scared of what you holding Ms. Tahiry!

It's just the gangster in me Skeet; that's all. Ha-ha! Tahiry you aint no gangster! See that Ko; he's gone make me prove my G! Kodi I'm not fooling with you two knuckle heads, my lil bro is on the way up, so make sure you guys order enough food for all of us when you get that room service. We got you baby! Thanks Kodi! Tah! What Ko? Are you going to place the order? Yeah, I'm doing it now! Oh ok!

Hold on Skeet, where are you going? To take a shower Kodi! I was just about to, can I go first; pleeassee! Sure go ahead! Ahhh look at Skeet; you pussy whip, aint you baby! Tahiry chill with that! Why; it's true aint it! Kodi makes her way in the bathroom as Tah and

Skeet go back and forth about her last comment while Ko just smirks and closes the bathroom door behind her.

I'm just messing with you Skeeta baby! Umm-hmm, when was the last time you talk to Meshaw? He's been calling but I never accept the collect calls. Damn that's cold Tah, why you do my boy like that? I'm done with his sorry ass Skeeta; I meant that! Alright calm down, I hear you Tah. Anyway; let's change the subject! How old is your little brother? He's 14! Cool, does he look like you? Yeah a light skinned version, my pops got a white lady pregnant.

Wow, ok then! Knock-knock! Knock-Knock! That must be him now! Oh shit, go answer it while I order the room service; I straight forgot! Yeah do that, order some fried chicken, steaks, rice, a pie and two bottles of champagne. Damn nigga; you got the munchies? Not yet but I will after we smoke these three blunts I got. Ooooh are you going to get your little brother High, Skeet! Knock-knock! Tah order the food! Alright, alright!

Hold on; I'm coming! Knock-knock! Who is it? It's me bro! What's up lil brother! Hey Skeet, damn! What's wrong lil bro? Who, who, who, the fuck is that! Hey there, this must be your little brother Skeet. Yep, would you please put some clothes on though Kodi! Hi-hi-hi-hi! Damn girl now, the lil nigga can't even talk! Aww stop tripping Skeeta, I'm sure your little brother done seen a naked woman before! Tahiry don't start!

She's right Skeet; what's the big deal! Tah order the food already, Kodi put on a towel or something. Lil bro have you ever seen a naked woman before? Yeah--yeah man! Was it in person nigga? Huh? You heard me boy? Umm, not really! Hold on, are you trying to tell me that my young brother is a virgin? Man I aint no virgin! Chill Skeet he's only 14! Kodi I was getting plenty pussy at that age. Tahiry now amused by the entire situation sits comfortably at the white marble kitchen bar, glass of wine in hand.

Kodi still naked, fresh out of the shower, takes a seat on the arm of the couch, slowly rubbing lotion allover - her soft, mocha colored skin, her legs agape and shaved vagina visible for all to see. Kodi come on now; are you serious! Skeet calm down, let the lil man look, it doesn't bother me.

Say bro, have you ever eaten some pussy, tasted a woman juices? Yeah man, I aint no rookie! See Skeeta, your little brother is bigger than you think! I think he's joking Tah. Well there's only one way to prove it, Skeet! Really and how is that Tahiry! Watch this; Ko want you let lil man eat your pussy, let's see if he has any skills. Why does it have to be my pussy Tah? Bitch because you're the one sitting there naked with your cat wide open! Just look at him, he aint stop looking yet, his lil dick is about to burst through them jeans!

So what are you waiting on lil brother, gone over there and prove it. He reluctantly pulls his hands from his pockets, looks at Skeet then Tahiry. What's wrong lil man, are you scared? No Ms. Tahiry. Well go ahead, she's sitting there waiting. Come on lil man don't be scared, my pussy doesn't bite. Skeeta's lil brother, slips off his shirt, slowly walks towards Kodi then lowers himself down to his knees and places his head between Kodi's; muscle tone, open, mocha legs.

Her juicy vagina, neatly shaved, glisten with water as she place her right pointer and index fingers over the top of her freshly clean pussy lips, slides them open then pulls his head in closer with her left hand. Kodi's eyes roll to the back of her head as lil bro's tongue softly but aggressively stroke her pussy.

Inside, up then around counter clockwise, his tongue went up against her sugar walls. Her loud moans echo through-out the hotel suite as Skeet look on with envy while Tahiry sit there salivating, wishing she were in Ko's place. Oh my God, damn you're eating this pussy! Holy shit! Slurp-Slurp-Slurp! Lil bro continues to suck and stroke, just as if he were tongue kissing his dream girl.

Damn Kodi, is it that good ho! Yeah bitch, hell yeah! Umm, damn I want you inside me, eat this pussy lil nigga! How old are you! Hmmm? I said- how old are you? 14! Damn I wanna fuck but you too young- oh-oh-oh-shiiiiittttt! Her back arches off the arm of the couch as she braces herself with her trembling arms; his head snug between her thighs.

Fuck that Ko, let him hit it girl! No Tah, I can't! Skeeta what you think; tell Ko to let him hit. Tahiry you're a freak, let him fuck you then. Skeet for real, go ahead man, they're in the moment. Lil bro do you think you can handle that pussy?

Umm-hmm! Kodi; do you want to? Skeeta I don't give a damn, somebody better put a dick in my pussy, fast!

Skeeta reaches in his back pocket, pulls out a condom then throws it over towards the engaged couple. Kodi pushes lil brother's head away from her vagina. Hurry, put on that condom and fuck me nigga! Lil man stands up, drops his jeans then slides the condom on his erect cock. Yes come hit it baby, hold on let me turn around! Ko raise up off the arm of the couch, turns around then bends over, her ass towards him. Come on, hit it from the back!

Lil bro, grips his Johnson, grabs Kodi by the waist with his right hand then slowly slides his snake inside her wet kitten. Uggghhhhh! Ugggggh! Damn, oh my! In and out, in and out, in and out he continues as Kodi screams sounds of intimate passion, Tahiry lustfully looking on as Skeeta skin boils with every daggering stroke. Oh shit, fuck me; fuck me, damn this dick is good!

Alright bro; that's enough! Back away! Skeeta hastily walks towards his little brother then pulls him away. What Skeet! Stop, that's what! Put your shit on, it's time to go! Ummmmm, damn Skeet, your lil brother can fuck! Shut up Kodi! Ha-ha-ha! What's so funny Tah! Yo Skeeta don't tell me you're jealous! Shut up Tahiry; put your clothes on bro it's time to go! Ha-ha! Kodi, look

Tahiry

Skeeta's mad! His young brother slides his jeans back on then his shoes then Skeet pulls him by the arm. Grab your shirt boy and let's go! You two get your shit together, we're leaving when I come back. Where are we going Skeet? Back to the A Kodi! Ha-ha! What's so funny Tah! Nothing Skeet, we'll be ready!

6. Dekalb County

"What's up A-Town it's a hot day in the A, it's going to be a turnt up summer baby." "This yo boy, J-boogie; on the one and only; Hot 87 FM!" "Here's some hot new wax, Gone to the moon from that boy Future, he got the streets on fire, right now baby!" "I'm gone to the moon" "I float like balloons" "I'm gone to the moon."

"Yeah, I smoke a box of blunts for breakfast" "Ay, and I woke up like Hugh Hefner." Hey Swayzee turn that radio down for a sec! What is it Tahiry? Yo, when am I gone get my Benz nigga; it's been three days now. Look shawty,

Spence said he was gone call me tomorrow after they replaced the VIN plates and get the title paperwork. Ummm, I can't wait to drive that pretty ass joker. Man all yall crazy as hell; you two are wanted by the damn police and you worried about a hot Benz, girl. Hold on Kodi, don't go there with me ho. I'm just saying Tah, think about it!

Girl you only live once; make it count; that's my motto! Now we're talking Tahiry; that's how G's think right there shawty. Man the way I see it, we're all going to jail anyway, so might as well enjoy life while we're free nigga! See, my boy Skeeta get it! Sway at this point, everybody in this damn Rover got it; let's just go get fucked up pimp! Let's get it poppin then Skeet, slang this right into South Dekalb Mall! Hydro smoke, fill the inside of the cocaine white Rover as Skeeta merges into the right turning lane on Candler road. Darkness falls over the parking lot of the South Dekalb Mall on the Eastside of Atlanta. Several cars await their turn to find a park in front of the Ultimate Sports Bar as swagged out fellas and Sexy ladies make their way through security and into the Ultimate.

Park right here shawty! Damn that's what's up; I aint even see that spot Tah! Yo put your tool under the seat Skeet, them boyz be searching you like you're in prison at this motherfucker. No doubt, I'm just ready to get some of

them wings! Me too shawty! Bring yall
greedy asses on, so we can get one of
those VIP sections. Hold your bra strap
Kodi; we're coming. I aint wearing one,
now what Skeet! Ha-ha! Girl you are a
fool! Don't laugh at that shit Tah, she
aint funny! No, what was funny was
your little brother breaking her ass off
on the couch the other day! Ha-ha!

Huh? What she talking about Skeet?
Nothing Swayzee, come on I need a
drink! Tahiry what were you talking
about? I'll tell you later Swayzee! Hello
people; welcome to The Ultimate, I need
to see your I.d's please. Here you go
shawty! Thank you Sir; enjoy yourself!
Here you go bruh! Thank you Sir, have
a good time. Look baby; we don't have

any pockets on these dresses but we are over 21. Where's your I.d's, ladies? In the truck! Ok, I'll let you two slide; this time! Thanks baby!

As the door open, loud music bounces off the walls amidst the patrons while they enjoy their food, drinks and each-others company. Black marble tile cover the walkway, complimenting the red couches, chairs and bar stools. Juicy J's; Bands A Make her dance play over the speakers as Swayzee, Tahiry, Kodi and Skeeta make their way up to a middle VIP section. "Bands A make her dance" "Bands A make her dance" "All these chicks popping pussy" "I'm just popping bands."

Hello guys, welcome to Ultimate, my name is Brittany and I will be your server. Hi Brittany, I'm Tah, this is Ko and those two fools are Swayzee and Skeeta. Hello yall, can I start you guys off with some drinks? Yeah shawty bring us two bottles of that Yellow Label. Ok sure, I'll be right back with two bottles of Veuve Clicquot. Thanks shawty! You're welcome!

"Bend it over, Juicy J gone poke it like wet paint" "You say no to ratchet pussy, Juicy J can't!" So guys you all know we have to move right, we can't stay off Covington no more. Tah what you talking? Swayzee we are wanted fool, what part of that can't you understand nigga? Shawty I aint scared to go to prison and I know my partner Skeeta aint either! That's you and his business but I aint feeling no jail cell Sway. Tahiry it's all part of the game baby.

Well I'm not with it, there's a dumb way to do things and a smart way. Look shawty; let's just have a good time right now, we can talk about that tomorrow, ok! Alright Swayzee- Girl, look! What Kodi? There's that fool that robbed me? Who, that pimp? Yep! Tahiry leans in closer to Kodi so she can hear her over the music. Where is he? Right there at the end of the bar, with that ugly ass orange derby on. Oh I see him, let me tell the fellas. Noooo, hold on, not yet! Why not Ko? I don't want any trouble, can we just have a goodtime. Are you sure Ko? Yeah, we can tell them later. Ok girl, if you say so.

Alright guys; here is your champagne! Let me sit your glasses on the table then I can pop a bottle and pour it up for you. Thanks Brittany! You're welcome Tah! As Brittany pour up the Yellow label, Tahiry keeps her eyes on Tiger as he makes his way through the club, networking and showing off his ho's. Her skin boils with disgust as she thought about what he had done to her best friend. Here you go girl. Tah! Huh? I said here you go; your drink! Oh, thank you Kodi! Um-hmm, where's your mind at? I'm good Ko, I was just day dreaming.

Tah I see you looking; just forget that punk; we'll deal with him later; enjoy yourself girl! Hey what you two over here talking about shawty? That's the pimp right there that robbed Kodi. Who, where he at! Is that him standing by the bar in that orange derby? Yep, that's him Skeeta! Hey, you girls chill; we'll be right back! Come on Sway, let's go handle this fool! What you do that for Tah! Girl relax, whatever he gets, he deserves.

Tahiry and Kodi watch from the VIP section as Skeeta and Sway make their way through the crowd in route to Tiger. Thick cigarette smoke, fog the air while white flashing lights form silhouettes every beaming second;

bouncing from patron to patron in the crowded establishment.

The closer they get to Tiger the slower everything seems to move. Tap-tap! Tap-tap! Swayzee; abruptly pokes Tiger on the shoulder. Yo what the fuck! Hey; you Tiger? Yeah who wants to know? We need to talk shawty; you got something that belongs to me. Look pimp, you need to back away from me, who you think you are! I'm Swayzee and you're about to find out who I am!

Bap! Tiger falls over the bar from the quick left that Skeeta threw. The crowd becomes anxious at the sight of the three guys fighting as Security rushes over to break it up. Tahiry wait! Where are you going? Stay there Kodi; I'm coming right back. Tah hastily walk down the VIP steps then heads outside. Alright busters; you knuckle heads got to leave, aint no fighting up in here!

Several guards grab Swayzee, Skeeta and Tiger by the arms and escort them towards the exit as Tiger's ho's stand there watching him as he gives them orders. Don't just look bitches, go get the car ready, get your dumb asses outside, now! Security stands in front of the door, holding Swayze and Skeeta back as they release Tiger. Come on man, this is messed up, let us at that fool! Calm down Skeet, yall don't need a charge, besides that boy aint even from around here!

Swayzee looks over at the security guard and shakes his head. Damn shawty I thought all East Side was supposed to stick together. Pow! Pow! Pow! Everyone hit the pavement at the loud sound of rapid gun fire. Pow! Oh shit; who's shooting! Skeeta shouts as he and Swayzee break away from the guards. Take that, you pimping motherfucker! Tahiry yells while she stands over Tiger's, warm, bloody body as his orange derby hat rolls down the parking lot. Oh fuck; Skeeta go get Kodi, we have to get the hell out of here, I'll grab Tah! Alright, get my gun from that crazy bitch and pull the car up!

Loud screaming; filter through the outside Decatur air as guys and girls alike run to their cars and away from the bar. Tahiry let's go! Swayzee grabs her by the arm then runs to the Rover, throws her in the back seat, starts it then speeds to the front just as Ko and Skeeta come out. Hurry, get in! Errrrr!

Tah sit quietly in the back seat as they speed off the South Dekalb, Mall parking lot, onto Candler road then hit the I-20 West exit towards downtown Atlanta. See Kodi, didn't I tell you I had your back. That pimp won't rob another ho, I can promise you that, Skeeta I need to smoke, roll me a blunt. I got you baby! Tah, the next time you plan on capping a nigga, how about let us know, damn! My bad Swayzee but yall was taking too long, forget that punk, aint nobody gone miss him anyway. Tah that was Gangsta! You like that Kodi? Hell yeah bitch, you did that! Yeah, that was clod blooded wasn't it! It was some Boss shit, you may be ready! Aww Swayzee, don't hate, just call me Boss, nigga, you know I'm ready! Ha-ha! Whatever Tah! We need to get off the street before this thing gets ugly.

As the blood in their veins slow to a normal pace, the adrenalin rush settles into reality. Tahiry's demeanor needed no words, her actions said it all as she slump back in her seat and gaze out the window at the Georgia Tree Line, along the interstate. A long quiet night of tossing and turning, would lay ahead; in a bleak hotel, just off Virginia Avenue.

Only God knows what the days ahead have in store.

Ring-Ring! Ring-Ring! Hello! Hey boy, wake your ass up! Who is this? It's Flawless, Skeeta! Oh what's up baby! Man where the hell you at; we been by your place twice already. Man we're over on Virginia Ave; you know we have to lay low. I heard about that bullshit; you fools must have a death wish! It aint even like that Flaw; where's my girl Stallion at! She's right here beside me! Tell her I said what's up! Stallion, Skeet says what's up! Tell that nigga I'm good. She says she's good! So what's the business man; we're trying to work at Follies today, yall coming through? Yeah we might do that, why you guys going so early?

Because it's paper in there during that lunch buffet! Hmmm, that means plenty of tricks too, huh. Yep, you got it Skeet and they be so fucked up you can hit them for all their cash. Me and Stallion be robbing those drunk fools. Alright bet, I'm gone handle some business then me and Swayzee will come through. Ok that's what's up babe, see you later. For sho!

Who was that shawty? Flawless and Stallion! What them ho's talking about? They want us to come through Follies in a bit. For what? Shit, they say its some cash in that joint during lunch rush and the tricks be wasted, early! Ok-Ok, sounds like my type of party, I'm surprise they aint ask you about that cash from that lick! Yeah me too, anyway, what time you wanna head out Sway? Give me an hour I need to run down to the courthouse. The courthouse! Yeah shawty! Swayzee what the fuck are you thinking about; you just robbed a bank, 5 days ago nigga!

Skeeta you worry too much, those boys don't even know it was me! Why they don't, aint your picture on the damn news. Shawty that don't look like me, besides if it did, I would be locked up by now! Man your ass is crazy! What you two clowns in here talking about?

Kodi tell this boy that the picture on the news looks like him. Hell yeah, because it is! Awww, Kodi you don't know nothing! Where's Tah! Sway baby girl has been tripping ever since she capped that pimp last night; she won't get out of bed!

Alright, stay here with Skeet; I'm going to check on her! Alright but she's not gone get up! Let me handle this Ko! Excuse me Sir; go handle it then! Swayzee walks out of the hotel room then across the hall to the room where Kodi and Tahiry slept. What you doing Skeet? About to clean this gun! Ooooh, can I watch? Yeah come on! You know guns turn me the fuck on! What doesn't turn your freaky ass on Kodi? Oh you got jokes! I'm just saying girl, you know it's true! Yeah funny, where is it? Right here!

Skeet opens his back pack then pulls out his silver 357 Magnum with the pearl handle. Damn it's pretty, is it loaded? Yep! Ummm, can I hold it! Sure, hold on. Skeeta slides the safety on then releases the revolver, turns it upside down then empties out the bullets. Wait- What! Don't take them all out, leave one in! Why? Please! Ok I left one in, now what? Close the revolver, remove the safety and sit back on the couch.

Hold on Kodi, what are you doing? Just trust me Skeet, sit back. I don't know about this Kodi, it doesn't feel right. Shut up and stop being a punk! She rubs her right hand over his Johnson, slowly, until it becomes erect then unzips his jeans. Damn Ko!

Skeeta relaxes, leans his head back on the couch as the warm sensation of Kodi's mouth move up and down his penis. The 357 lay beside them on the couch while Skeet right hand embraces its white pearl handle with a firm grip. Umm, damn you got some good Georgia Dome girl! Put it to my head! Hmm? The gun; put it to my head! Kodi stop fooling around! Skeet, stop being a punk and do it! She reaches over with her left hand, grabs his forearm then slowly guides the gun to her left temple.

Slurp-Slurp! Slur-Slurp! Shit Ko what you doing- damn your mouth feels good girl! She lifts up to speak. Pull the trigger! Huh? Pull the trigger Skeet! Ummm, damn you crazy Ko! Puulll iiittt! Ugh-ugh-I can't! Ouch! Why you bite me bitch! Pull it! She slides her wet lips back down his cock while looking up at him then over to the gun. Click! He jerks the trigger. Oh shit girl, damn you're crazy! That was close! Puull iiitttt again! What! Puuullll itttt aaagain!

Skeets hand tremble as she continue to stroke his penis with her juicy lips, the soft white light above gleamed off the polished chrome barrel. Ummmm, oh my God woman! Puuullll iiiit! Click!

Tahiry

Uggghhh! He sighed as the adrenalin flow through his body from the thought of the 357 hammer dropping on the firing pin. Slurp-Slurp! Slurp-Slurp! The stroke of her tongue going up and down made his knees shake but the fear of the bullet piercing her brain kept him on edge. Slurp-Slurp! Ummm, Kodi shit, I think I love you girl! She looks up at him, with her pretty brown eyes then slurs a few words. Puuullll iiiiitttttt, pulllll the triggeerrrrr! Reluctantly he grants her wish. Click!

"Good Afternoon Atlanta, this is Patsy Downs, reporting live from Decatur." "As you can see I am standing in front of the Ultimate Night club a very popular hang out here on the East side of Atlanta." "Last night a young man lost his life, right here in this very spot." "If you look closely, you can still see the blood stains on the pavement."

"The Dekalb County Sheriff still has not released the name of the deceased because they are still trying to contact the next of kin." "If anyone seen or heard anything, please call the tip line, now located at the bottom of your screen." Officials are still searching for clues as to who committed this horrible crime."

Tah get your ass up; what you doing shawty! Chill Swayzee, my fucking head is killing me. Then turn that damn TV down. I was listening to the news;

they were just talking about us. Tahiry them fools don't know shit, if they did, we would be locked up on Memorial in the County right now, shawty.

Yeah whatever man, I aint going to jail! Tah you just dropped a nigga in a public parking lot, what the hell are you thinking! And you robbed a damn bank with no mask on, now what! See shawty, that's the difference; I don't give a damn about going to jail. Three hot's and a cot baby, it's just college for criminals that's all it is shawty. Well, have fun in the pokey by your damn self; I'm laying low.

Hey, do you Tah, I was just checking up on you, Ko said you were depressed.

Sway I aint hardly depressed, especially not from dropping that punk ass pimp. Now can you please get out of my room and close the door behind you. Slow down shawty, we're about to head over to Follies in a few; you wanna roll? Nah I'm Gucci, maybe next time. Alright; be easy Tah, we'll be back soon. Yeah; umm-hmmm, close the door behind you.

Ring-Ring! Ring-Ring! Hello! Listen, you sorry ass excuse for a man! You aint shit but a sperm donor! Charlene, don't start that bullshit! Why weren't you at court Swayzze! I'm on the way shawty, did I miss it or something? Yep the judge pushed it back to 2 O'Clock! 2 O'Clock when? Today nigga! I'll be there Charlene; that's an hour and a half from now. You better bring your black ass down here Swayzee, you such a damn bum! Bye Charlene; I'll be there! Click! Swayzee! Swayzee! I know that jack ass didn't just hang up on me!

Sway looks at the time on his cell then hurries out to the Rover to head downtown to the court house. Ring-Ring! His phone rings just as he glances. Hello! Man where you at? Hey Skeeta; I'm on the way down to the court house! Sway you are a crazy ass nigga! Why am I crazy, Skeeta? Bruh; you and Tah are all over the news and you got the nerve to pull this! Shawty I told you them fools don't even know that it's me, I'm gone walk right in that court room,

328

hear what the judge has to say and leave. Just Crazy; that's your problem boy, aint no damn judge in their right mind gone let you walk free!

Skeet just chill shawty, I'll meet you guys at Follies later. Ok Sway, if you say so! I'll be there shawty, just save me a seat, you know them damn Mexican's be having shit on lock over on Buford. I got you bruh! Cool, I'm about to pull up to this court house. Alright Sway!

As Swayzee makes his way out of the parking garage, past the Marta station, up the sidewalk then into the Dekalb County Court House, a chill came over his body as he got closer to the metal detectors. Sway places his wallet, keys and loose change inside the plastic, blue tray on the scan belt. As he walk through the detector then exit on the other side, the hall leading to the court room, though only a few steps away, he thought seem longer than before.

It's about time you get here, you sorry son of a bitch! Hey calm down shawty; why you tripping? Can I walk in the court room first girl! Charlene aggressively places her right pointer finger in Sways face as they're walking in. You should have been here three hours ago, Swayzee! Well, I'm here now Charlene! Yeah whatever, I know you better have some money or your black ass is going to jail today playa! Girl I just gave you 500 dollars two weeks ago, did you tell your punk ass attorney that!

500 dollars! Boy I don't know what you're talking about! Go ahead with them games shawty! You aint give me no money Swayzee. Oh ok, that's how you want to play it! Yep! Alright bitch, then I'm asking for a DNA test, the lil nigga probably aint mine no way!

Court room patrons sit in awe as the two continue to argue while walking down the aisle as the Bailiff watch with concern. Excuse me, excuse me! What man! You guys need to be quiet, sit down and have a seat. You can go ahead and lock him up officer; the judge is going to do it anyway! Ma'am; please go take a seat. Yeah, take a seat skank! Sir that's not necessary please have a seat on the other side.

Shawty I'm not sitting no-where, anyway that ho can kiss my ass! Charlene turns back around, faces Swayzee, looks into his eyes then raises her voice as loud as it could go.

You just need to pay me, my money-Smack! Smack! Swayzee before he knew it; raises his left hand then pops his baby momma across the face two hard times. Ouch! Did you see that sir, he smacked me! The Bailiff reaches for his Taser gun just as Swayzee takes off running out of the court room. Hold it right there Sir or I will have to tase you! Fuck you shawty and that ho, I aint paying shit! Tell the judge, I don't give a damn. Hold it, right there! Swayzee backs up towards the Court room doors then makes a run for it.

As Swayzee enters the hallway, he sprints back to the front of the building; darts pass the front desk officer, through the double glass doors, down the cement steps, up the sidewalk then to the parking garage, out pacing the bailiff. Sway jumps in the Rover then speeds out of the garage, breaking the yellow and black parking arm then into the traffic of downtown Decatur.

Ring-Ring! Ring-Ring! Hey Sway; where you at? They aint lock your ass up! Hell nah Skeet I had to sprint out of that bitch shawty, I slapped Charlene's slack ass! You did what fool! Man, she was mouthing off, I aint got time for that bruh! Boy you crazy, I'm pulling into Follies, you coming? I'm on the way shawty, order two shots of that 1800! Alright bruh see you in a bit, them hoes here already too, I'll just wait outside until you get here. Cool are they working or what? Yeah, they shaking! Good, I need some strippers in my life right now, shit is out of control. I feel you Swayzee, see you in a bit bruh! Bet!

Damn Stallion, we should have gotten here earlier, it's too many bitches in this damn dressing room. Flaw; forget those ho's, hurry up and get dressed so we can get some shots; I need to get my mind right girl, my car note is due. I'm coming Stallion, hold tight; let me tie this hair up, or do you think I should leave it down? It looks better down to me babe! Ok cool, I'm ready then, let's go get this paper.

The notorious venue, occupied with shake dancers from all races smell of hot fried chicken, mac and cheese, meat balls and cigarette smoke. Its runway style stage display sleek silhouettes of gorgeous women, amidst the hundreds of customers and other dancers; under the dim, black and green fluorescent lighting.

Tahiry

"Gentlemen welcome to Follies, the sexiest adult club in Atlanta!" On the left stage we have Miracle, Brittany's on center with the lovely Fancy on the right stage." "Please help yourself to our lunch time buffet and don't forget to get yourself; a half off table dance and if you really like the lady that's dancing beside you, go ahead and get a private dance." "I promise that you will leave a satisfied customer!" "I'm Dj Rick and it's time to jam with some 2 Chains!"

"I'm riding round I'm gettin it, I'm riding round I'm gettin it." "I'm riding round I'm getting it." "It's mine I spend it." "It's mine I spend it!" "I'm riding round I'm getting it!" "I'm smoking on exotic my girl aint got no stomach."

Stallion and Flaw stand beside the bar awaiting their shots while scoping the club for marks. Umm, come on Flaw there's two tricks right there! Where Stallion? Over in front of the bathroom bitch, move your ass before these thirsty ho's get over there first. Oh I see em! Flaw and Stallion head towards the two Latino Gentlemen standing by the wall outside the restroom.

Hey fellas, you two want a dance? Sure mommy, what's your name? I'm Stallion and this is my girlfriend Flawless. Oh your girlfriend huh? Yes that's what I said. Umm, so why don't you kiss your girl for me then? How much? How much what mommy? You can call me Flawless poppy and how much are you going to pay to see me kiss my girl?

Damn mane; you charging for that? Yes I am! Ha-ha! The other fellow laughs then just stand there admiring Flawless beauty as she goes back and forth with his friend. See, your homie even laughing at you; this is a strip club baby; everything cost! Alright Flawless, you better stick your tongue all the way down her fucking throat too mommy. Oh I'm gone tongue her good, how much are you giving me? Here you go; One hundred dollars. Absolutely not! Make it two hundred poppy! Damn mane; you greedy! No babe; Flawless don't work for free, now pay up!

Mane, you killing me here! Thank you! Stallion bring your sexy ass over here bitch! Flawless snatch Stallion by her right arm; pulls her close then slowly grabs Stallions head with her right hand then glides her long juicy red tongue down Stallions deep throat. I yi-yi, I love this shit! Let's go get a shot and do that again, this time we want a dance! Ok poppy, anything you want, let's find a table!

Smoke clouds, cascade over the entrance as Swayzee and Skeeta finally make their way inside, pauses to take it all in then scans the room. Yo shawty, there those ho's go right there, by the bathroom. Oh I see them, let's grab some drinks while their working. Good idea Swayzee, I got the first round. Cool, order me a double shot of that 1800. Alright I got you, lord it's some pussy up in this motherfucker. You never lied about that, Follies is the lick. Damn sure is, look at all these drunk tricks, I got to jack at least one of them fools for their shit Sway!

Skeeta I thought you knew, that's the only damn reason I came, fuck them stinking ho's, a nigga needs to get paid shawty. Swayzee you aint said nothing I don't already know my nigga. Bartender! Yeah baby, what can I get you? Get my partner a double shot of that 1800 and I want a double shot of that Patron Silver. Alright baby, coming right up, did yall want something to eat? We got a free lunch buffet going. Yeah, where are the plates? There over on the table baby, yall go ahead I'll save your seats! Thanks shawty! You're welcome.

Skeeta, we been sleeping on this damn place shawty. Look at all this pussy, tricks, free food, man this is a thug's paradise. Hell yeah, I know we can get 15 to 20 stacks out this bitch, easy! Yo I'm robbing me a fool before we leave Skeeta, know that! Yeah I know but I'm about to kill this macaroni first. Ha-ha! I feel yah Skeet; I'm just getting a few wings, I'll see you back at the bar.

Yeah mommy, shake those chi-chi's! Oh you like that huh poppy? Yes, I love it mane. Well just sit back in the seat for me, so I can give you a good show. Anything for you Flawless, you're my new wife mane. Ha-ha! I don't know if you have enough money to afford me poppy. Money is not a problem mane; me and my friend are rich mommy. Oh yeah; what is it that you guys do? I own a landscaping company and my friend owns a gas station. Damn, hold up, did he just say a gas station Flawless? Yeah bitch, he did.

Simultaneously, Flawless and Stallion straddles each guy's leg then slowly grind their vagina's on their knee caps while staring lustfully into the gentlemen's eyes. Umm poppy, don't you want a private dance? No mane, let's go to my place, how much is it going to cost Flawless? It depends poppy! On what? If your partner wants to fuck Stallion or not, we give a discount price when you book both of us.

Are you kidding me mommy, of course he wants to, who wouldn't! Stallion, are you down with that? What baby? Doing a double tonight! As long as they're paying, I'm laying baby! So, when and where poppy? Tonight mommy about 11! Ok we can do that poppy. How much is it going to cost mane? $600 each poppy! Oh now Stallion speaks! Ha-ha! He got jokes Flawless! Nah mane, she aint said two words the whole time but since we're talking about money, now she speaks. Ha-ha! Leave my girl alone.

Bruh this mac and cheese is on point! This chicken aint bad either shawty, are them hoes done over there yet though? Nah, they're still up there in that corner with two Mexican's! Oh I see em, I wonder if they got some cake. They better have some Sway, fucking with Flaw and Stallion thirsty asses. Ha-ha! You aint lying about that right there Skeet! Hey I'll be right back Sway, those niggas look like they're about to go to the head.

What you doing? I wanna know if they got some paper bruh. Oh ok, hurry your ass up before they come back then. Yeah, yeah just chill nigga. Skeeta walks away from the bar then up the steps, makes a left then heads over to Flawless and Stallion. Hey boo; what's up? Hey Stallion, Flaw! So what's the move, yall hanging with us tonight? Yeah; after we go on this date with these two Mexican's.

So what up with them though, are they holding? Hell yeah, them fools own like a gas station and shit. Oh word! Yep! You bullshittin Flaw! Stallion tell this fool, I aint playing. Yeah it's true! Bet, so set that shit up then so we can hit them fools, you know how we do. Ok just let us take care of these dates then we can case everything up. Hold up

Stallion; Skeet what's up with that scrilla from that house lick, yall aint even paid us for that yet! We got you Flawless but yall need to get these two clowns drunk now, we're gone rob those fools before they leave.

Man you wildin! I'm serious Flawless, make it happen, Swayzee ass is too hot to be playing around in them streets. We got to get it while it's hot baby. Alright, alright, go back over to the bar and wait, I'll signal yall when it's time. Now that's what I'm talking about Stallion, get your gangster on girl. Bye Skeet, get on before they come back! I'm gone, I'm gone, slow your roll Flawless.

Knock-knock! Knock-Knock! Kodi, open the door! Knock-Knock! Knock-knock! Kodi! Where the hell is this girl? Knock-knock! Tahiry paces back and forth in front of the room door as she impatiently waits for Kodi. Knock-Knock! Bitch, answer the door! Knock-knock! Hold on, hold on, I'm coming Tah! It took your ass long enough! My bad girl, I was in the shower. Swayzee said we all are supposed to be going to Follies. Yeah girl, they're at the spot already, Sway met Skeet over there after court.

So what's up then Ko, you rolling or what? Look at you ho, just a few hours ago I couldn't wake your ass up, now you wanna go party! I don't know about you Tahiry, you got issues. Kodi put some clothes on and stop talking so much and I wasn't sleep I was thinking. About what? Getting some more cash, what else! Hmm, I was thinking maybe that pimp was on your mind. Who, that Tiger chump! Yeah, isn't that bothering you? It comes with the game, right Kodi, besides, that nigga robbed you.

Damn girl, you didn't have to kill him. Yes I did Ko, he had to be stopped. I'm glad you're my friend because you crazy. Ha-ha! Kodi hurry your ass up, I'm hungry and why are bullets sitting on the coffee table? Oh those are Skeeta's; he took them out of his gun while I was giving him head.

Huh? Run that by me again, why would he have his gun while you were blowing him? Tahiry pauses in front of the room door, slides both her hands into her back jean pockets then leans forward with a puzzled look on her face. I'll tell you in the car, come on let's go, I'm ready. Ha-ha! Kodi you're a freak, I can't wait to hear this one! Shut up Tah, come on.

More and more customers pile into Follies over on Buford highway for the fine women and good buffet as Skeeta and Sway sit at the bar plotting their next move.

How's everything baby, did you want another drink? Yeah I'll take another.

Hey bring me one too! Sure hun! So what's the word Skeet? The girls say them guys are loaded, they own a gas station and some other shit. Oh, we're hitting them fools before we leave here shawty, for show.

I'm down Sway but we aint got no guns bruh. Yo, we just have to rush them fools, catch them in the bathroom so we can strangle their asses or something. Man we need to think this one through Sway; it's a lot at risk in here. You right Skeet, let the girls get them wasted then we can see what happens. Alright bruh, I got to get me a few dances though, it's some fine girls in this motherfucker.

I'm with you on that one Skeet! Ring-Ring! Ring-Ring! Damn hold that thought Swayzee; I need to get this. Ring-Ring! Hello, this Skeeta, what's poppin? Yo what up, yo folks told me you had some things to get rid of. It depends on what you're looking for! If I can make a profit off of it, I'll buy it. What you got? Some Art, some watches, silverware and some jewelry. That's cool right there, I'm downtown at the Marriot, when can you come through so I can take a look at it? Shit, we can be there in 30 minutes my nigga.

Bet it up, hit me up when you get here I'm on the 12th floor. For show, see you in a few. Who was that shawty? That's the call we've been waiting on! What call? Ol boy, the one that's going to buy that lick! I feel you, when he wanna get it? In 30 minutes bruh; later for them ho's; we can get at them later, besides we don't need to rob them fools now bruh, money is waiting on us.

Let's ride then shawty! Hey bartender, here you go, keep the change! Thank you baby! Damn Skeet, why you leave that hoe 50 dollars! Man chill, let's go.

7. Pay up

Ring-Ring! Ring-Ring! Yeah, what up shawty? What happened to your ass last night Swayzee, me and Ko went to Follies and yall punk asses wasn't even there and you niggas didn't even answer your phones! Chill Tahiry we had to handle some business, where you at right now anyway? None of your damn business! Click!

I know this damn girl didn't just hang up on me! Ring-Ring! Sway I got a date, bye! Tah- Click! Knock-Knock! Knock-Knock! Hey hun, come in! Hi Tahiry, you're looking sexy. Thanks honey, how much time did you want to spend with me?

All I need is thirty minutes baby, you can drop those pink panties and ly on that bed, open them legs and let me lick that clit for you. Oh really, I don't let strangers eat my pussy boo. Come on baby, I promise you'll love it. I'm sure I will. How much are you trying to spend? Shit, fine as you are, I'll drop 800 just to taste that pretty thing.

Well, in that case, go over there to the sink and wash your mouth out with that Listerine on the counter. You don't have to tell me twice baby. Good, I'll be sitting right here waiting, so hurry up before I change my mind. Ummm, I'll be there in a sec!

He rushes over to the sink, grabs the mouthwash bottle, opens it up, gargles, spits it out then grabs a small white towel from the rack, dries his lips then drops to his knees and slowly crawls over towards Tahiry's spread eagle, creamy thighs.

Come here nigga, and lick this pooh nanny! I'm coming baby, I'm coming. The bright white beam of light from the street lantern outside of her hotel room window, cast his shadow on the plain, egg shell white walls as he crawl closer to his prize. His huge shadow; impedes her open legs as their bodies, shadow dance upon the ceiling. Tah's back arches off the chair while lustful chills run through her sugar walls then up her spine. The trick's nose rest firmly on her pelvis as his tongue strokes her clit simultaneously while holding a mouth full of pussy.

God damn it boy, you're eating the fuck out of my vah-jay-jay, you a freak! You gone lick my ass too! Ohhhh shit! He swiftly moves his tongue from her pussy down to her butt hole then back up to her clit again. Slurp-Slurp! Slurp-Slurp! Slurp-Slurp! Boy I need to be paying you for this, damn it feels so good! Slurp-Slurp! Slurp-Slurp! Umm-hmm! You got to stop; it's supposed to be about you. Slurp-Slurp! Slurp-Slurp!

Don't worry about me baby, I'm paying to eat this. Umm-hmm; and you can put that 800 dollars on the table too, baby. God damn nigga, you can eat some pussy! You like that mommy! Umm-hmmm, where's my money, get up and let me ride that thing.

Ok hold on; let me get your money. Yeah do that, while I get a condom. Oh shit, I done fucked up! What's wrong baby? I forgot to go by the ATM; I don't have any cash on me! Ugh-uh honey, what the fuck did you just say!

Yo, yo, calm down sexy, I'll just run down the street to the bank, I'll be right back! Hell nah fool, leave me your Driver License or something. It's in my car Tah! You better leave something nigga or you aint walking out of this room- Bam! Oh no this motherfucker didn't just run out of here! I can't believe this just happened, aint this some bullshit! The money green carpet, pastel designs and dingy wallpaper in the hallway all seem to blur together as the trick ran at full speed to the end of the hall then through the stairway doors as Tah's voice echoes around him to stop. Disgust dawns her face as she stands in the now empty hallway butt ass naked with her cell phone in hand while the trick gets away.

Ring-Ring! Ring-Ring! Hello, who is it! Damn ho, calm down! My bad Kodi, I'm pissed the fuck off right now. I can tell, is everything ok? Yeah I just got played by this simp ass nigga. What happened? Kodi I don't even feel like talking about it, where you at? About to walk in Skeeta's place. How about you ask that fool why they weren't at Follies when we got there last night! Oh I already found that out Tah! Really? Yeah they went to sell that stolen shit out of Swayzee's trunk. Well you better get in there fast because those idiots will trick that cash the fuck off, if you don't stop em! Girl I'm already on it, I'll talk to you later, here's Skeet!

Alright I'll come through in a bit! Cool, see you later than Tah! Hey Ko, how long you been standing out here? For a minute! Why you aint knock then, I heard your voice that's the only reason I came to the door. I was on the phone with Tahiry, what you doing? We in here counting this scrilla! Damn, you told me that an hour ago when I called you, yall still counting. Man hell yeah, Swayzee dumb ass aint had no sleep last night; that fool keeps dosing off in the middle of the count.

Come in, you want something to drink; there's some Ciroc on the counter. Nah I'm good baby, hey Sway! Hey Kodi, what's up girl? Ha-ha! Not yo ass! That shit aint funny, Skeet come help me finish counting this cash shawty. Bruh just take your ass to sleep already, me and Ko can finish the count. No, no, no, aint no bitch touching my money! So what are you trying to say Swayzee? I just said it.

Kodi don't pay him no mind. Skeeta; that's two duffle bags full of money right there! Where did all this come from? We had it stashed at our safe house but it's not safe there anymore. Especially since the cops are after Sway and Tahiry's ass. Skeet I hear yall talking about me and Tah, shawty; I aint sleep! Man I want to see some ass, let's grab a few stacks and go over to Pin-Ups!

Swayzee you the most tricking nigga I know, no wonder you can't keep no money. Skeet get yo bitch! What you say Swayzee- Calm down Kodi, it aint that serious. Baby we're on the run from the police and probably the FEDs. We don't have time for no bullshit Skeeta! Kodi just shut the fuck up and sit down, can you do that for me, damn! Alright I'm sitting but yo boy's a big trick baby, that's all I'm saying. Why in the hell do yall keep jacking fools, if all yall gone do is spin it on strippers! Kodi, if you say another word, I'm gone kick you out. Skeet you better not! Then shut up! Ok, ok.

Swayzee move your ass over so I can finish the count. Damn shawty; don't push me off the couch! Bruh just move over or take your ass to bed, we need to finish this count so we can get the hell out of here.

Come on baby, I'll help you count it; Swayzee's too sleepy. Yeah it's all of that damn weed he smoked! Kodi takes a seat on the floor in front of the coffee table by the money. Two blue gym bags, unzipped with stacks and stacks of dirty money inside, sit on the right side of the table as they both retrieve it, one bill at a time, placing rubber bands around every thousand dollar bundle.

Skeet! Yeah what's up Kodi? Now you can buy me those Red Bottoms I wanted. Girl stop being greedy and count this money. So you're not going to buy them! Hell no, all that hoeing you do, buy your own. Alright, the next time you want some head, you gone pay for it nigga. Aint no thing, I rather pay for it, that way I don't have to go through this bullshit. Zzz! Zzz! Zzz! Look at yo boy, he cutting tree's over there. Yeah never mind his ass, just keep counting, we don't have all night.

Skeet you're not gone keep talking to me any kind of way. Kodi can you please chill, damn! Whatever, where did yall get all of this? Shit most of it came from that fence. What is that? Somebody who buys stolen shit, I told you that already. Oh yeah you did, what about that bank money? It's in there too. Knock-Knock! Knock-Knock! Damn, who is it! It's Tahiry, open the door! Ko go let your girl in. Ok!

Hey girl, what's up? Hey Tah, we're counting this cash. Damn, that's a lot of scrilla! Hey Tah! Hey Skeet, is my cut in there? What cut you talking about? For that bank job, I was the driver, remember. Shit I don't know, I guess so! Don't worry about it; I'll just take my cut. Hold on a minute Tah, you better wake Swayzee up.

Dude, you must have forgot that I'm running shit. Ha-ha! Tah you my bitch, tell him again. Look Tah, that's on you, I aint in that! Umm-hmm, I'll take six of those stacks, Kodi hand me those bundles right there. Here you go girl. Thanks and you lucky I don't take more Skeet, have yall heard from oh boy in College park yet? Who? My Benz, remember! Oh yeah, we're picking it up tomorrow. Cool, I'm gone run across the way to my place to pack some more things while yall finish counting. Ok Tah!

Tahiry tucks the six bundles of cash into her blue Gucci bag then heads for the door. Don't take too long Tah! I won't Ko; what the- Hey is Swayzee and Skeet in? Damn, yall scared me! Yeah they here; whose asking? I'm Flawless and that's my girl Stallion. Oh I heard about you two; yeah them fools in there. Skeet! What Tah! You got company! Who is it!

It's Stallion nigga! Oh hey, come in! Hey Skeet! Hey Flaw! Damn, how you counting money and you aint call us. I was gone call you when we got finished counting. I bet you were and who is this bitch! Excuse me! Hold on ladies, be cool, this is my folks, Kodi. I don't mean to be rude Kodi but Skeet why is she touching our money. Wait a damn minute; you need to turn it down horse, Stallion or whatever your name is; don't try me Bitch!

Look, everybody needs to calm the hell down. Stallion all of this didn't come from you guys' job, I got you guys' cut right here, just be patient. Go grab a beer out of the fridge or make a sandwich or something, damn. Man I don't want no sandwich, give us our money. Flawless please get Stallion. I got her Skeet, we cool. See, I told you Flawless, that's why I drove over here, I knew these fools was going to cut us out. Well, we're here now and we aint leaving without it. Zzz! Zzz! Damn Skeeta, he knocked out aint he! Umm-hmm.

Knock-Knock! Knock-Knock! Damn who is it now! Kodi check the door! Knock-Knock! Police, open up! Knock-Knock! Dekalb County Police; open the door or we're kicking it in! Oh fuck! Swayzee! Swayzee! Swayzee! Zz! What! Wake up bruh, the cops outside! Oh shit where! Outside nigga! Knock-Knock! Bitch, grab some cash and let's go, forget these fools Flaw, come on I'm jumping out of the bathroom window.

Stallion and Flawless snatch some cash off the table then run to the bathroom. Knock-Knock! Police, open up!

Get that bag Skeet, follow them ho's, jump through the window, come on Kodi! I'm right behind you Swayzee! Bam! Bam! Bam! The door knob shakes as the hinges come undone from the heavy force the cops thrust upon the door. Bam! Bam! Bam! The white molding separates from the doorway and splinters as the wooden door slams to the carpet. Bam! The Dekalb County Police enters the premises, guns drawn, on a now empty apartment. The silk white bathroom curtains blow in the wind from the open window. Trails of 10, 20, 50 and 100 dollar bills lay on the living room floor, in the hallway and the bathroom tile.

"It's empty guys; get some cars to search the complex they can't be too far." Roger that chief!

ANTWAN BANK$

8. Tension

Flashing blue lights from Dekalb County Police cars, mirror in the dark tint of Tahiry's Black Mercedes Benz as Spence slows to a cautious speed while driving pass the officers on Wesley Chapel road as they ticket an irate driver. Ring-Ring! Ring-Ring! Spence calls Sway from his cell as he yields for a red light at the corner of Wesley Chapel and South Hairston to make a right turn. Off to his right two homeless men hastily approach the driver side window. Ring-Ring! Ring-Ring! Hello!

Yo what up Swayzee, I'm about 2 miles from your crib, about to drop Tahiry's

371

Benz off. Damn I just left shawty! Where you at Sway? Going down South Hairston; about to cross over Redan road! Tap-Tap! Hold on Sway, these damn bums tapping on the fucking window. Alright! Tap-Tap! He rolls the window down. Yeah what's up?

Click-Click! You know what it is nigga, get out the damn car! Oh shit, hold on playa, you don't want the car, here I got some cash right here man, about three stacks! Man get the fuck out, this is my last time telling you! The other bum, stand behind his friend nervously as cars roll by. Hey Spence! Spence! Swayzee yells out his friends name as he hears the confrontation over the phone but to no avail.

Pow! Pow! I told you to give it up nigga, now your ass is dead, get the fuck out! He grabs Spence lifeless arm as his partner runs around to the driver side then jumps in while he toss the bloody body in the street, jumps in the car and spins off. Spence lay there taking his very last breath with the cell phone still in his right hand as Sway screams for him. Spence! Spence! Errrrrr! Bam! Sway unknowingly releases his foot off the break and hits the car in front of him. Oh shit!

I'll be damn, I don't believe this is happening! An elder gentleman steps out of the damaged car just in front of Swayzee. His dark brown, wrinkle skin swung from his elbows just under his yellow Polo shirt as he slowly inspected his 99 olds mobile for damage. Looking over his glasses, he raises his right brow as Swayzee approaches him. I'm sorry Pops, I was on the phone talking to my friend as someone just car jacked him and shot him while I was on the phone. I didn't mean to hit you sir!

The old man, grabs hold of his khaki's by the belt loops, pulls them up a bit then starts to speak. I'm sorry to hear about your friend young man, why don't you give me your insurance information, I'll call the police to go check on your friend and we can get all of this ripe mess taking care of. Swayzee pauses then thinks about what the old man just said but quickly jumps back to reality. Yeah hold on, I'll get that info for you, stay right there! Suddenly he remembers the two keys he stashed in the back of the Range. Sway makes his way to the back of the truck, grabs the two packages then runs down the hill of the Kroger's shopping Square parking lot, looking for anyone he might know.

Over in the corner; he spots one of his High School class mates walking away from the barber shop. JD! JD! Swayzee what up fool! Hey my nigga, I need a quick favor! Calm down boy, what's up? Yo hold on to this for me, I just got into an accident, I can't have this shit on me. What is it, looks like a damn microwave box to me. Shawty there's

375

two keys in here, just hold it bro and I will look out for you. Man, I aint trying to get in no shit! Shawty it's mine, you good, I promise I got you! Alright nigga, two days that's it! Thanks shawty, I got you!

Yeah nigga, now get your ass back over there before you bring that heat over here. Yeah for sho, thanks shawty! Swayzee starts to run back up the hill, feeling a little better but not really, he still had to deal with Spence but there was no time, the cops was just pulling up as three more flew by going in the opposite direction.

At the top of the hill he could see the old man pointing at him from below as two cops look on. Sway turns around and quickly walks inside the grocery store, contemplating his next move; he removes his black T-shirt then wonders down the frozen vegetable isle wearing his white wife beater, Tru Religion jeans and Air Max sneakers. The immediate pressure of the current events weigh heavy on his mind, time was running out and the cops, surely was on the way down that hill.

Swayzee walks over to a young man reaching in the freezer for a pack of corn on the cob. He notice the blue and red, Atl baseball cap on the teenagers head then reaches in his jeans pocket and pulls out a fold of twenty dollar bills.

Hey shawty! Hey shawty! Yeah what's up folk? I'll buy that cap off you man, here's 300 dollars! Shit, you can have this motherfucker, here you go! Thanks shawty! Swayzee places the hat on his head, pulls it down to fit snug, just over his eye brows then heads for the exit while reaching for his cell phone.

Just outside of the double sliding glass doors, two Dekalb County police cars pull in front of the entrance as Sway calmly walk up the sidewalk then up the hill to Redan road. Ring-Ring! Ring-Ring! Hello! Hey Skeet, man I just fucked up, I wrecked the Range and the damn cops are looking for me! Man where you at? Over on Redan about to jump on the Marta, pick me up at

Stonecrest Mall. Alright nigga, lay low, I'll meet you there. Coincidently the Marta pulls up just as Swayzee gets to the bus stop; he could see the cops still searching for him, one standing inside the grocery store entrance as the other cruise the parking lot.

So Bitch, you are not going to believe what just happened! What are you talking about Kodi! He aint tell you! Tell me what girl? Well, I was lying on the couch with Skeet watching TV when Swayzee called. Ko if you don't tell me what the fuck is going on; I'm hanging this damn phone up. Damn girl, I was gone tell you that Spence got shot while he was driving your Benz! What! You heard me! Where's my car! Some bums stole it!

Girl; don't play games with me! I'm serious they shot that nigga in the head, left his ass on Wesley Chapel and drove off with your shit! Aint this some Bull; I can't believe my luck is this bad. I'm sorry Tah but- But what? It's Karma girl. Aint such thing Ko, Spence should have been packing. Tah that's cold, you didn't mean that. The hell I didn't, that was my car, I stole that shit myself. Bitch a nigga is dead and you talking about a car. Ko it's like Swayzee said, it's all a part of the game shawty.

Yeah whatever, Skeet is going to pick up Swayzee now, are you coming to the room? In a little bit I have a date on the South side; I'll head over after that. Alright that's what's up, see you in a bit.

Kodi walks over to the Hotel room window; that overlooks Virginia Avenue. Homeless people, College Students and bar hoppers scroll the busy sidewalks as a constant flow of cars and trucks come to gridlock while behind the Marta Bus. The AC hums as it blows a fluid scream of cool air through-out the room. Merlot wine colored carpet cover the room floor wall to wall. Egg shell white wallpaper overlay the century old sheetrock walls. The heavy tan painted, metal door; sit ajar, joining the two rooms together. A soft piercing female voice, echoes from the flat screen television immediately grabbing Kodi's attention.

"Hello Atlanta, this is Breaking News!" "Dekalb County Sheriff's Department has released these four photos. They say that these four individuals, known on the streets as Swayzee, Tahiry, Kodi and Skeeta are wanted for involvement in an ongoing crime spree." "Official say, they are responsible for Grand Larceny, Grand Theft Auto, Homicide, Prostitution and Breaking and Entering." "If you have any kind of leads or information regarding the where-about of these dangerous persons please call the local authorities." "Police are asking that you do not try to apprehend these individuals, they're considered to be armed and dangerous." "I'm Kenya Morris; reporting live for your 5 O'Clock news."

Oh know the fuck they didn't! I can't believe it! Kodi panics, paces back and forth in the room as she ponders what just happened. Her heart began to beat five times its normal rate as her hands starts shaking sporadically. Kodi's life as she knew it was coming to an end, in awe, she slides down the wall then on to the floor, her knees to her chest, head nestled in between.

She finds it hard to dial Tahiry's number on her cell while her finger's steadily shake. After a few seconds, Kodi calms her nerves then makes the call. Ring-Ring! Ring-Ring! Yeah Ko, what's up? Girl you need to get over here, now! What's wrong Ko! All of us are wanted by the police now, not just you and Sway! Stop talking crazy, you aint do shit! Well I just watched the news and their looking for all of us; they even said that we were armed and dangerous! Damn, is Sway there yet? No, I'm about to call them now! Alright do that, I'm on the way! Ok bye!

Ring-Ring! Ring- Hey Kodi, what's up baby? Skeet where yall at? Turning on Virginia Avenue, why what's up? They had you and me on the news with Tah and Sway! What the fuck! Yeah we're wanted too, the whole damn city is looking for us now man! Fuck, we'll be there in a sec! Where's Tahiry? She's on the way; is Swayzee ok? Yeah he good! Ok, see you guys in a minute, we need to fix this shit! Yep!

Man, Kodi said they had all of our pictures on the news as being armed and dangerous! Quit playing shawty! I'm serious Swayzee! Damn that aint good, we need to get back to the Eastside shawty! We need to do something nigga, Tah is on the way back to the room; we all need to put our heads together on this thing.

Skeet speeds up Virginia Avenue, past Spondivits then over the bridge, through the light then makes a right into the hotel parking lot. They come to a hard stop, pulling into the first empty parking space they see, jumps out of the car, runs through the sliding doors and down the hallway as the front desk attendant looks on with concern.

Hastily he turns around then grabs the phone off his desk as Swayzee and Skeet wait for the elevator. Ring-Ring! Ring-Ring! "911, what's the emergency!" Yes I think I see those people you had on the news in my hotel. "What people would that be sir?" The two girls and two guys that are wanted for that crime spree! "Ok sir, please give me your address and don't try to contact or apprehend the suspects!" "We're showing you at the Quality on Virginia Avenue, is this where you saw them?" Yes Ma'am, they're staying on the 6th floor! "Ok are you a guest or are you an employee?" I'm the front desk clerk and Manager. "Alright just keep calm; we are dispatching some units out now." Yes Ma'am thank you! "No problem Sir, help is on the way!"

Errrrrr! A bright yellow, four door Taxi; slams on its brake's just in front of the Hotel's entrance just as the Clerk hangs up the phone. Tahiry's red, six inch stilettos; expose her pretty manicured toes through its open toe while coco-butter glisten off her bronze skin. Her fitted red dress left no room for the imagination as it hugged her every curve. Clinching her blue

Giuseppe bag tight; she rushes to the elevator as the clerk look on.

Ding! The elevator door opens and Tah quickly steps in, heart pounding fast and mind spinning a million miles a minute. Ding! She reaches her floor, runs off then enters the room where the others impatiently await. It's about damn time shawty, we have a fucking problem! Nigga who are you yelling at! It's because of your Bitch ass, that we have a problem!

Fuck you Tahiry! Don't get mad now Swayzee; just shut up and let me figure this thing out! Baby girl it aint no getting out of this one, we just need to head back over to the East side where our folks at, this room is getting hotter by the second. I'm sure it is Skeet but we need to know what our next move is going to be, before we go running back to Decatur! Well I hope you think of something soon girl, I'm scared as shit right now! Calm down Kodi, it's going to be cool, just chill for a sec. Yo check this out shawty, we got a stash house over behind that BP off Wesley Chapel, we can hide out there for now. Is it safe Swayzee? Yeah Tah, we got look out boys on the payroll, we good shawty!

Tahiry takes a long look at Swayzee, sizing him up as she ponders her next move. Alright nigga, we can go there but we're going in separate cars. Girl we only have one damn car! Well you and

Ko take your car Skeet and me and Sway can catch the cab over. Bet it up, let's go Ko, I need to pick up some weed before we get over there anyway. Tah hurry up, are you sure yall gone be straight in that taxi? Yeah girl, we'll meet yall over there. Ok cool! Get yah shit Ko and let's roll! I'm right behind you Skeet baby. See you two fools in a bit, I'm gone pick up some loud then I'll we'll be right over. That's what's up shawty! Look Swayzee, I sure hope this spot aint hot! It's safe Tah, trust me! Yeah I heard that before!

Damn, you're looking sexy as hell in that Red dress right now though! Sway, get your things and let's go before it's too late! Shawty I have everything I need, and all you want! Nigga, your ass will probably bust a nut as soon as you look at this pretty pussy of mine, come on, let's go! Ha-ha! Yeah, I'm gone hit that, yep you want me. Ha-ha! Come on fool the Taxi's waiting; time to get the hell out of College Park! Lead the way sexy!

9. Karma

Skeet why are you taking the Covington Highway exit! We are supposed to be going to Wesley Chapel! Chill Kodi, I'm just gone stop by the gas station to pick up some loud from my partner over on South Hairston, right there by the crib. I don't think that's a good idea baby, you know our faces are all over the news! Nah we good girl, we're on the East side, aint no thing baby.

Well just hurry up so we can go meet up with Swayzee and Tah before she starts calling me, you know she's crazy!

Yeah, yeah calm down, it's just two more blocks up the street.

As the daylight fade away and the night begin to set in, hundreds of headlights beam across the South Hairston and Covington Highway intersection. Loud music from several cars parked at the car wash and near by gas pumps, echo sounds of local Artist; T.I, 2 chains and Future. The Covington street light turns green, yielding the South Hairston traffic while Skeet cruises through the light then makes a right into the gas station parking lot.

Look there's my partner right there as always. Just hurry up Skeet, I really don't think we should be here anyway.

Kodi you worry too much; this won't take long at all. Skeeta parks in the very last parking space on the left; just in front of the store. His partner stood at the corner of the building, just left of the entrance. The aroma of marijuana got stronger the closer he got to his partner.

Yo what up Skeet! Hey bruh, I need a zip. Oh for sho, I got two zones left. That's what it is; let me get both of them. Alright how much you got shawty? I got you playa, you know me. Yeah, show me the cash first Skeet. Kodi sit in the passenger seat worried as she looks on while the two men conduct their business. Man I told you I had you- Yo don't try and play me Skeet!

The dope boy stands his ground, eyes wide open, reacting to his gut feeling. Skeeta reaches in his jeans pocket with his right hand while reaching behind his back with his other. Pow! Pow! Skeeta's limp body collapses down to the pavement in front of the store entrance as he yells out, gurgle in his voice. What the fuck! I told you not to play me Skeet! He leans over Skeets body, places the nose of his nine on Skeets forehead then pulls the trigger. Pow! Just then he notices a black money bag in Skeets left hand as he lay there bleeding out.

Nooo! Nooo! Nooo! Kodi screams out as she jumps from the car then runs up to Skeet's dead body. The Dopeboy, realizing what he had done, takes off running across the busy South Hairston highway as patrons look on, some with cell phone camera's out while others call for help.

Skeet! Skeet! Skeet! Baby, get up! Get up! Please don't die Skeet! Please don't leave me! She pulls his warm body up by his shirt as the blood ooz onto the pavement from his wounds. Ring-Ring! Ring-Ring! His cell phone goes off as he ly there. Kodi reaches over his body, picks up the phone to answers it but stops as police sirens sound in the distance.

Reluctantly she pulls herself together; kiss him on the forehead and runs back to the car. Ma'am, where are you going?

Get away from me bitch, I have to get out of here. What about your friend! There's nothing I can do for him now lady, he's gone! The eye-witness; looks on in disbelief as Ko puts the car in reverse, speeding away from the scene, crying with Skeet's cell phone in hand.

Ring-Ring! Ring-Ring! Hey Skeet; where yall at shawty? Swayzee! Swayzee! Is this Kodi? Yessss, yessss! What's wrong, where's Skeet? He's dead Sway! What! He's gone! Bitch quit playing and put my nigga on the phone! He's dead Sway, that dopeboy killed him! He's gone! I saw the whole thing Swayzee, he shot him right here in front of the store. Kodi get your ass over here right now, you need to tell me what the fuck happen! I can't-I can't! I can't right now- Click! Kodi! Kodi! Kodi-, dammit! What's wrong Sway? That was Ko, she said Skeet is dead, this some bullshit! What! She said that lil nigga that slang at the corner store by our house, popped him! Nooo! Nooo! Is he gone be ok! Tahiry; I just told you my nigga is dead shawty! Oh my God, what are we going to do! We need to go check this shit out and find your girl too! Driver, turn this taxi around and take us over to Covington Highway and South Hairston! Yes Sir, no problem!

Meshaw Gardner! Yeah; what the fuck you want! Don't raise your voice at me inmate! Roll up your shit, you going home. C-O; stop playing man! Gardner you got 5 minutes to get your ass out of this cell or you can stay another night! Hold on C-O; I'm coming, I thought you were bullshitting! Meech rises up off his bunk; slips on his blue inmate top, jail house slippers then grabs his books and letters off the cement counter top. Is that all you got inmate! Yes Sir! Alright let's go! Meshaw hastily exits the cell then follows the guard through the module exit door, down the narrow hallway then into the out processing staging area.

Alright Gardner have a seat right there on that bench, the booking officer will be with you in a minute. No problem C-O but can I ask you a question? Yeah what is it? What happened, why am I getting out? Don't ask me son, the Chief says to release you, we release you. Damn, tell him I said thanks. Gardner, just sit your ass down and wait for the officer. I aint about to deliver no message to the Chief!

Damn bruh, ok! Gardner! Yes Officer! Here are your clothes; you can go in that bathroom to change. Man for what, yall done had me changing in front of these niggas for almost a month, aint no difference. Suit yourself, get dressed. The officer tosses the large clear zip lock bag across the counter to Meech. Bet it up, a nigga about to be out of Dekalb County, yall foul in this bitch, aint no love! This is jail son; we didn't put you in here. Love is for those you left on the outside. Yeah, where is my money and jewelry? Thump! There you go! I see you like throwing things! Meech slips on his jeans, T-Shirt, sneakers, necklace then ring. Yo can I use your charger officer? Nah! Come on bruh, I need to call me a ride. Alright 5 minutes! Thanks bruh!

Hey what is this? It's a check! I see that but where is my cash. We have to return all cash back in the form of a check. Damn are you gone cash it? No sir, but you can go to the check cashing store right down Memorial, they will be glad to. Man yall something else in here. Meech takes the officers charger of the counter then plugs it in the outlet beside the bench, waits for it to come on, then makes a call.

Ring-Ring!   Ring-Ring!   Ring-Ring! "We're sorry but the person you're calling has a voicemail that hasn't been set up yet." Aint this a bitch! Skeet, be on that bullshit. Let me call Swayzee ass. Ring-Ring! Ring-Ring! Ring-Ring! Yo who this! It's me nigga! Yo you got your phone in the pokey shawty! No fool, I'm out; where you at? Man Skeet just got shot; I'm on the way over to the corner store by our spot. Quit playin Sway! I'm serious shawty, me and Tah in the Taxi headed there right now. Taxi! Yeah man it's a long story!

Alright I'll meet yall over there, tell my baby I said what's up! That's what's up shawty, see you in a bit. Who was that? Meech! What the fuck you mean, Meech! He just got out and he's going to meet us at the store, he said to tell you hey too. What in the hell, how that punk get out Sway, he got to be snitching, it aint been a month and he supposed to be looking at a 5 year bid. Yo that's yo man; yall can discuss that shit when you see him. Right now we got to check on Skeeta! You should call Kodi, we need to know where she's at; besides she seen everything too. You right, let me call her ass right now. Ring-Ring! Ring-Ring!

Hello! Hey girl, where are you, you ok? No I'm not ok Tah, I fucking seen everything! Oh my God, I'm about to go crazy! Kodi calm down baby, tell me where you at so I can come be with you sis. I'm on Candler road. Where on Candler Ko? Behind the Dairy Queen! Girl; are you crazy, them niggas thirsty over there! I just need to be alone Tah, I can't believe he killed him. Look I'm hurt too baby and I don't want you to be by yourself while you're feeling like this. Click! Kodi! Kodi, Hello! Damn, she hung up! Call her back Tah! I am nigga, chill! Ring-Ring! Ring! Ring-Ring! Man she aint answering this phone, we need to get over to Candler Sway! Alright, we can go after we check on Skeet! Swayzee, this is fucked up-

****

On the East side of Atlanta, just off Candler Road and a block from Panthersville Road, patrons crowd the area restaurants along the block as two Dekalb County cruisers followed by one black unmarked car turns right on the side street between Dairy Queen and Wing Stop. Cheap $20 whores creep up and down the sidewalk trying to catch a date as low level dope boys wait on the balcony of their destitute hotel, scoping the area for their next sale.

Knock-knock! Knock-Knock! Who is it! Hey shawty, you got a smoke! Get away from my room door! Damn shawty, I stay right next door, I just want a cigarette! I don't smoke! Ok then my bad, what you doing over here, you working? What you mean? Come on Shawty, this here the trap, either you slanging dope or pussy. Which one you selling? Why you asking? Shit I can use some good Georgia Dome right now, since I can't get no Newport! How you know I aint the police. Shit I saw you when you checked in, you aint no police. You look like you running from somebody to me. I aint runnin! Oh yeah, open the door then, I got some cash. How much you got? Man I got 20! 20 what nigga? Dollars shawty, it's just head girl. Yo get your ass away from my door, before I cap your ass! Damn bitch, it aint have to be like that!

JUST FUCKING LEAVE! Ok, ok, ok I'm gone, damn! You broke

motherfucker, stay away from my room. Ring-Ring! Ring-Ring! Damn, a bitch can't even sit here and grieve! Kodi, exhausted, scared and uncertain of her next move, looks down at her phone and see Tahiry calling again. She picks up the phone then sends the call straight to voicemail.

10. Culmination

Several police cars, along with a fire truck and ambulance sit in front of the crime scene on the Gas station lot. Traffic crossing the Covington Highway and South Hairston blvd slows to see what's going on as Tah and Sway pull up in their taxi. Ok sir, do you want to get out here? No shawty, just chill and keep the meter running. A light drizzle adds to the already gloomy scene. Red and Blue Emergency lights bounce off windshields as they beam through the night air.

Damn, I can't see nothing Tah; can you see Skeet? Nah I think he's in that ambulance. Fuck, we can't get out, this is bull shawty! Let's just go find Kodi, Skeeta is gone Sway. Hell no, I need to know for sure and if he is cause I'm gone kill that nigga who shot him!

Hey look, there's Meech walking up right now! Can we just go already; I don't have anything to say to that fagot! Hold on Tah, I'm gone call him and tell him to check that ambulance. Oh my God, just hurry up Swayzee. Ring-Ring! Yo man, where yall at? Hey Meech, we're in this taxi, parked over by the pay phone. What, I don't see no pay phone. Man look to your right, I'm looking right at your ass. Ok I see yall, get out the damn taxi and let's go check on Skeet. Shawty we're wanted by the damn whole city! Bruh why the hell did you come up here then? Meech just go ask one of those medics if Skeet is dead or not. Alright Sway I'll call you back!

He pauses for a few seconds and observes the scene. Three detectives lay white numbered placards on the very spot where Skeet's body left its blood stain. Two police officers tie off the area as the team began their investigation. Reluctantly he makes his way over to one of the medics standing at the rear of the ambulance who was removing his sky blue, bloody latex gloves.

Excuse me bruh! Yes Sir what is it? That guy in your truck is my friend, is he going to be ok? No Sir, I'm afraid not, he was D.O.A. Damn; there wasn't nothing you guys could have done for him? I'm afraid not Sir, sorry for your lost. Meech takes a deep breath, looks at the medic, nods his head then walks back over to the taxi.

Here comes Meech, damn I hope my boy is alright! He doesn't look happy Sway; don't get your hopes up. Swayzee rolls down his window as Meshaw approaches. So what did he say? Skeets gone bruh, he was dead when they got here. FUCK! Look while you two are sitting here getting mad I need to find Kodi, she doesn't need to be alone right now. Yo take the taxi and go get her, I'll wait here with Meech.

Tahiry

Hey dumb ass, as soon you get out of this cab them cops gone lock your black ass up! I'm not going to jail! Yo I parked at Publix; the taxi can drop us off over there. Bet; get in the front seat. Hey shawty take us to Publix, right across the street! Yes Sir, no problem.

Hey Tah, how are you doing? Turn around Meshaw and don't talk to me, I have nothing to say to your punk ass. Damn baby, I said I was sorry! Yeah you are that and how in the hell did you get out! I bet you snitched on somebody, didn't you! Girl cut all that non sense out, aint nobody, no damn snitch! Whatever Meshaw! I miss you Tahiry that's all. You should have thought about that before you decided to cheat on me with that ho. Tah; the girl was on the computer, I aint even fuck her for real. Well you might as well have fucked her, it's just the same. Ok we're here, Publix! Yo just pull up to that white Camaro, right there in front of the bank. Camaro, what bitch let you drive her car? Stop tripping Tah, that aint no bitch car. Whatever; just get your ass out Meshaw!

Yo Tah go find Ko and call me when you find her, we're going to find that chump she said shot Skeet. Who shot him Sway? Lil shawty; that slung at the store right there! Who, that fool we bought our loud from? Yep! Man I'm gone merc that fool, come on; I know where he be at! Meech and Sway jump out of the taxi then walks to the white Camaro. Tahiry don't forget to call me shawty! Go get that nigga Swayzee; I got this! Meech; your bitch is crazy! Tahiry leans over the seat to address the driver. Hey honey; take me to Candler road; right by 285. Yes Ma'am!

Again Tahiry find herself silent and gazing out of the window as the driver speeds up Flatshoals in route to Candler. She collects her thoughts then tries to call Kodi once more as they get closer to the block. Ring-Ring! Ring-Ring! Hey Tahiry, I'm fine. Don't give me that BS Kodi; which one of those traps you in? The one in the back, Tah! Damn bitch, you would pick the most dangerous one, I'm turning in now, what room you in? 223! Alright be there in a sec! Hey man, make this right then another right then go all the way down the hill, she's in room 223 on the back side.

As they cruise down the hill, guest from the opposite hotel, look on from the balcony trying to see who was in the taxi. Dude you need to speed up, I don't know these folks back here and you better hall ass as soon as I get out. These niggas back here will kill you for $20! Yes Ma'am, I hurry! Yeah you better, how much I owe you? The whole trip is $200! Damn, what in the hell are you charging me for, a trip to Miami.

Tahiry

No Ma'am, we came from College Park to Wesley Chapel to Covington Highway and now Candler road. Oh that is right, here you go, now get out of here and thanks for driving us all over the place. You're very welcome, it was my pleasure. Tahiry steps out of the cab, walks up the sidewalk then the stairs and makes her way to room 223. Knock-Knock! Knock-Knock! Suddenly the room door opens and Kodi stands there, pain written all over her face as she try to hold back her tears.

Awwww, come here girl. Tahiry grabs Kodi then holds her tight while the tears stream down her face. It's gone be alright girl, just trust in God and he will lead us. I can't believe he's gone Tah,

416

my baby gone. That motherfucker just shot him for no reason; Skeet wasn't even trying to shoot that boy! All he was trying to do was buy some loud Tah, that's all! Shhh-Shhh. God got him baby, God got him.

Where's is Swayzee, why aint he with you? He stayed with Meech; they're gone to find that kid who shot Skeet. Meech, what you mean Tah? Oh that fool got out somehow. Ko removes her arms away from Tahiry, wipes her eyes, regroups then looks in Tahiry's eyes. He out, did he snitch? I don't know girl, all he said was, they let him out and he aint no snitch.

What the hell is all of this on the table Ko? Powder, what it look like. I know you wasn't gone snort all this shit! Yes and I still am, I need to get my mind off this, I just keep seeing Skeet laying on the sidewalk and that nigga shooting at him. Damn, that is fucked up; come on, I'll do some lines with you.

Kodi grabs Tah by her right hand then leads her over to the table. I need this right now Tah and thank you for coming! You know I got your back girl. Where did you get this from anyway? It was under the driver seat in Skeet's car.

10 year old, rust colored carpet, cover the room floor and smelled of mildew. Pastel print, wall paper; hang loosely

from the walls as the AC unit under the window blow the chocolate brown curtains from below. Years of smoke, steam and hand swipes, left permanent smears on the bathroom mirror. Future's; Same Damn Time play in the background from Kodi's mobile phone as they sit at the table snorting nose candy together to ease the pain of Skeet's death. "I wear Gucci, I wear Bally at the same damn time" "On the phone, cooking dope, at the same damn time."

Ko leans over the shabby table, places her nose into the pile of cocaine then takes a hard snort. Ahhhhhhh! Go ahead Tah, get some! Hold on bitch; let me move my hair out of the way, this natural, I can't have no coke in my shit. She ties her hair back, leans over the sugar hill then takes a hard snort with one finger over her right nostril. Umm-Umm! Damn, this is strong girl! No cut baby-no cut! What, you trying to kill us ho! Shhhh! Be quiet Tah, just enjoy this high, ooh you feel it, yes take me away! Please take me away!

Kodi, I don't feel a damn thing! Just wait a second, it will hit you, relax. Yeah I feel it now, I can't hit that no more; I never felt like this. Don't it feel good though Tah? Umm-hmm that's why I can't do it no more, my ass will be hooked. I don't do it that much Tah; I just need something to calm my nerves. You wasn't there girl, I saw that boy shoot my baby down, right on the motherfucking sidewalk in front of that store! I can still see it Tahiry, plain as day, plain as day- Ring-Ring! Ring-Ring! Hold that thought Ko; this is Swayzee. Ring-Ring! Hello! Hey you find Kodi? Yeah I'm sitting with her now. Good, we found that fool who capped Skeet, get yall shit and come to the Budget on Panola! Are you talking about the one over behind that BBQ place? Yeah that's the one Tahiry, hurry up shawty, we need Ko to pin this nigga.

Ok, ok we coming, what room yall in. Come to the back, we in 234! Alright; we're leaving now! Bitch where the keys, we got to go! Where we going Tah! Over to Panola road, Sway and

Meech found ol boy that shot Skeet, they need you to I.D him. What, they got him? Yeah girl, come on! Both ladies jump up, still high from the coke, snatch their purses then run downstairs to Skeet's car. I'm driving Kodi, give me the keys. Here, drive I don't care; just let me at this nigga! Calm down Kodi, I need you to be thinking clearly when we get there. If this is him, I'm sure Sway will let you put in work. The girls jump in the car then speed over to the Budget.

A few miles, several turns and a couple of exits later, they enter the Budget Hotel parking lot. 8 stories of rooms, tower over the I-20 interstate, yellow tape blocking some rooms could be seen from afar. Pimps, Dope Boys, Ho's and Junkies pay weekly fairs to call this place home. Fresh crime scenes only last a day before the rooms go back available again, a common practice at this trap. Tahiry and Kodi cruise to the rear of the Hotel then park in front of room 234, exits the vehicle then runs upstairs to the second floor.

The Air condition unit in the $37 room, sounded off like a lawn mower while the Television blast from its highest volume. Meshaw and Swayzee stand over the little dope boy from the corner store, while he sat tied up in the one wooden chair that sat at the table. Dingy, White Ripped twin bed sheets, wrap his torso like a mummy, bounding him to the chair with no clothes on underneath as Sway patiently load his 357 revolver.

See shawty, word on the street is, you the jitter bug that capped my boy Skeet! My man Meech right here just so happened to get out of the pokey today and when I told him who you was; he brought me straight to your punk ass!

Now this fool been locked up for almost a month and he found you! Shit, I don't see how you call yourself a hustler, living up in this dump. Bruh I didn't shoot your boy, why would I do that, yall buy weed from me like every other day! Bap! Meshaw turns then back slaps their hostage. Shut up punk!

Skeet's girl seen the whole motherfucking thing and she's on the way! So you better start praying because if she says that you're the fool that shot him, Swayzee is going to put a bullet right between those big ass eyes. Then I'm gone shoot you in the Heart!

Man come on Meech; you know me bruh, I aint do it. Bap! Shut up fool or I'll smack you again. Sweat drip from his forehead and onto the sheets that wrap around the chair and his torso. The ball cap on his head began to get wet around the edges from the sweat that perspired from his cranium. His heart rate increase every second as he sat there hopeless, not knowing what his future held. Look Sway, yall on the news my nigga! Meech shouts as he watches the TV.

"In tonight's Evening News, police are still searching for these dangerous individuals whose aliases are as follows." "Starting from the photo on your right, my left; this young lady goes by Tahiry, the one next to her goes by Kodi, both are known to be working the local Escort trade and are also wanted for questioning involving; murder, robbery and grand theft auto!" "In the next photo, this guy is known as Swayzee, authorities say he is no stranger to crime and will shoot on site, he has no respect for police or any authorities!" "And tonight; right before this broadcast, we were notified by

Dekalb County Police that this man in the last photo was gunned down on the East Side of Atlanta just a few hours ago. He went by Skeeter!" "Officials still have no clue on the where abouts of these criminals but ask that you be very careful and to call 911 at first site!"

Man they didn't even mention anything about who killed Skeet, that's bullshit! Calm down Swayzee, yall fools are wanted! You know what; fuck it! I can't wait no more Meech, I'm wasting this chump right now, I aint waiting for Kodi no more! No Swayzee, please! Please! Don't shoot me!

Sway chill, what if he didn't do it! So what, we'll go find the shawty that did it! Man that don't make no fucking sense, just calm your crazy ass down, the girls should be here in a minute! Thanks Meech, don't let him kill me! Bap! Boy shut the hell up! Sway; give me that sock off the floor. Here you go shawty, what you gone do with that? Meshaw takes the sock, turns it inside out until it forms a ball then stuffs it in the hostage's mouth. Here nigga! Ummm-Ummm! Now we don't have to hear his bitch ass mouth. Knock-Knock! Knock-Knock! Who the fuck is it?

Open the door Meech and stop fooling around! Hey yall, come in! YOU, YOU, YOU MOTHERFUCKER- THAT'S, THAT'S HIM SWAYZEE! THAT'S THE NIGGA THAT SHOT SKEETA! WHAT!

YOU SHO KO! HELL YEAH! Immediately Swayzee places the barrel of his 357 to the dope boy's forehead. POW! Meshaw reaches behind his back, pulls out his nine then points it straight to the dope boys heart. POW!

Oh my God, we need to get out of here, fast! Calm down Kodi, where the hell are we gone go! Anywhere but here Tah, I can't be beside no more dead bodies. Yo everybody just take a second and think about this for a minute. You, you and you are wanted by the police, I'm clean. So what the fuck are you trying to say Meech! All I'm trying to say Tah, is let me make the next move, I can find a safe place because my face aint hot. Yeah whatever Meshaw, how you get the fuck out anyway! You aint had no bail; you violated your probation and got a new charge for hitting me, so please Sir! Tell me, how in the hell are you standing here in front of us right now!

Baby chill with all that nonsense, I aint no snitch, if that's what you saying! Umm-hmmm, what the hell ever, if it walk like a duck and look like a duck, it's a damn duck! And you're looking like that Aflac motherfucker to me right now, Meshaw!

Meech, I swear if you're the cops, I'm dumping on you shawty! Swayzee you know me, come on bruh! Bam! Bam! Bam! Who the hell is that knocking like that? I don't know Kodi, go see! Uh-uh. You go see bitch! Bam! Bam! Dekalb County Police, open up! I knew it, I knew it, I told yall, you a snitch ass nigga Meech! Hold on Tah, be quite! Be quiet for what Meech, you told them we were here! Oh shit Sway! Sway hold on bruh, put that gun down! Bam! Bam! Police, open up or we're kicking it in! Bam! Bam!

Yo I aint going back to jail shawty! Sway no! Tah yells as he points his gun towards the door! Bam! Bam! Fuck the police, I'm Swayzee bitch! Pow! Pow! He lets off two shots towards the door. All went silent, inside the room and out, everyone pause to see what was going to happen next; did he just shoot a cop.

Click-Click! Pow! Pow! Pow! Pow! Gun shots enter the room from the opposite side of the door. Kodi turns and try to make it to the bathroom for cover as Tahiry dives on the nasty floor between the Twin beds. Pow! Pow! Sway let off two more bullets then ducks beside the bed to reload. Pow! Pow! Pow! Pow! More bullets riddle the windows and door as the cops release an-on slot of ammunition inside the room.

Pow! Pow! Pow! Meech return fire while ducking for cover but the amount of artilery coming from the other side of the door was too much. Meshaw, Swayzee, Kodi and Tahiry did not make a sound as the bullet riddle door creep open, pillow feathers float in the air, along with wall dust from the pierced sheet rock as the officers enter the room with guns still drawn. Alright, anybody moves and we're putting one in your damn head!

The hostage body, sit in the middle of the room, white sheets now bloody as his body began to slump forward. Over on the floor, lying in front of the sink, Kodi lay facing down as one of the police officers approach. Ma'am, Ma'am can you hear me? No response. He kneels down on the floor beside her, places two fingers on her neck, waits a few seconds, looks up at his Captain then shakes his head to say no.

Tahiry

Lying on the bed, face up, eyes wide open with the 357 in his right hand; Swayzee's face held a cold, dead stare as blood roll down his left cheek from the wound in his forehead. A soft moan along with a cry, caught the officers attention as they lift Meshaw's, heavy dead body off of Tahiry as she lay there curled up in the fetal position.

The Captain, grab her by the arms, stands her to her feet then sits her on the bed. Miss Tahiry, we've been trying to catch you guys for some weeks now, why didn't yall just turn yourselves in Ma'am? Look around, now all your friends are dead. Puh! Tahiry hawk spits, right in his face. That's it; read Miss Tahiry her rights and take her down to County! Yes Captain! "Ma'am; you have the right to remain silent. Anything you say can and will be used against you in a court of law. You have the right to an attorney. If you cannot afford an attorney, one will be provided for you. Do you understand the rights I have just read to you?"

Thanks for reading Tahiry; the 11th release from ANTWAN 'ANT' BANK$. We really appreciate your support; please be sure to leave a review and remember to tell a friend. You may also read more titles from Antwan Bank$ and any of the other PRINTHOUSE BOOKS Author's. All titles are available anywhere that books are sold and reviews can be read on our website.

MADE; the Epic Crime Thriller Trilogy.

Three years ago, I lost my wife and family to this messed up economy. After that nothing was there to hold me back, with no more support from Uncle Sam; I decided to pave my own way. Never one to break the law, I traveled down the straight and narrow but to no avail, thanks to this Bitch ass Cop; name Espinoza. So again I found myself in a corner. But as I gathered my thoughts and tried to come up with a plan; it was by fate that I met who would later become the love of my life.

Sabrina in her own fortuitous way introduced me to the life I have today. Still no wife nor kids in the picture, even though they constantly held a place next to my soon to be cold heart. I witnessed my life change in a split second. Now that I think back on it; mine did that very day I dropped Pharoah's punk ass in that back parking lot. I should have known things would never be the same after that day. I still get a thrill when I think about the look he had in his eyes when I took his life away and the smile that remained on Sabrina's all that day.

As I sit here smoking on this Cohiba, in this Mansion, with all this power, all this money and all the blood on my hands from those fools that stood in my way. My heart still beats fast at the sight of the cars, money, houses, women and the sound of hot bullets piercing warm flesh. See I live for this shit because there's nothing else out there for me; but this. Don't blame my mother, don't blame my pops. Blame Uncle Sam for placing that M16 in my hands and brain washing me to kill without feeling a damn thing. Blame this messed up economy; that has so many people struggling. Yeah I made a choice and I am happy with it. Because of that; me and my crew will protect what's ours until the day we die. See we don't plan on going to no prison, jail or nothing like that. Yes we plan to go out with a fight, last man standing! Death before Dishonor; that's how we roll! Gangsters make the world go round and Sin City is its axes.

ADORATION: *Love Unconditional.*

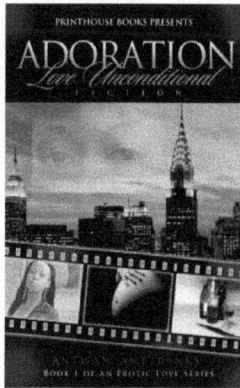

The word Adoration can be defined as fervent and devoted love or simply put; to worship. During our time on Earth we will all experience this powerful thing called Love. This novel will take you on a journey seen through the eyes of four couples and their relationships. For Love we endure amazing things and some of us will go to the limit to keep it.

Love can fill your heart with joy or leave it filled with hate. Adoration explores love at several levels; some of them good; some bad. In Book One of this Series; hearts will break, tears will fall, blood will shed and bells will chime; all in the name of love.

Suite 206; An Urban Crime Short.

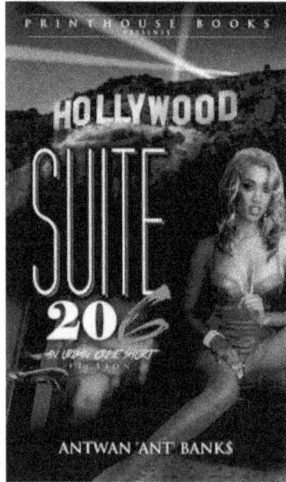

Millions travel to the City of Angel's every year in search of that one shot at stardom. But most fail and find themselves caught in the underbelly with the homeless, the drug attics, prostitutes, thieves and murders. Candy and Joe unfortunately are no different than most and end up living in a different hotel every other night; doing whatever needs to be done just to survive.

The Cover Girl Series: Miss Jones. Book 1

The Cover Girl series is about, an Atlanta; Eye Candy photographer; name Malakhi Jones. Pronounced (Mal uh Ky). This short story and many others to come; will take you inside a day in the life of a hot photographer and his daily encounters with several of the industries sexiest Magazine Models and Video Vixens.

While these events are Fiction; anyone in the industry knows; what goes on at the shoot; stays at the shoot! Malakhi is at the top of his game. He is connected with every Mens Magazine Publisher, Casting Director, Hip Hop Artist and Talent Manager in the industry. Getting a session with him is like winning the lottery; when it comes to being an eye candy Model, in the ATL. Any Model knows; that once the session starts and that camera flashes; all rules will be broken to obtain that success; if not! Then keep dreaming.

The Cover Girl Series: Lola Love. Book 2

ANTWAN 'ANT' BANKS

In book 2 of The Cover Girl Series; Malakhi ventures on an on location shoot, with the Sexy Chocolate, Video Vixen; Lola Love. Her enticing aura almost proves to be too much for the A List Photographer but in true Malakhi fashion; he prevails. The two meet up, downtown on

ANTWAN BANK$

Peachtree street Atlanta; at one of the Cities five star hotels.

Together, they will create magic for the camera and hot lustful memories in their Jacuzzi Suite. They say a picture is worth a thousand words but only the photographer and the model knows; what exactly goes on, between those poses.

F.I.T.H. Fear Influences Thine Heart

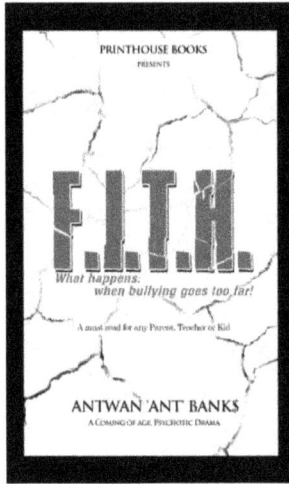

Earlier in the mid 80's and early 90's; I had the unfortunate opportunity of being friends or acquaintances with two special individuals. Now that I am thinking about it, maybe it wasn't unfortunate but faith that we crossed paths. Their stories we're similar, even though they happened at different times and in two separate parts of the world.

It is through my God given gift that I will deliver their message; through Eric; F.I.T.H's main character. I find it my destiny to help others see life as they did; at tragic moments in both their lives. The time and location of events and names have been changed to protect them and their victim's families. Hopefully this story will show why it's not cool to be a bully but deadly, when you factor in all the consequences.

The Party Life; 179 of My Favorite Cocktail
Recipes

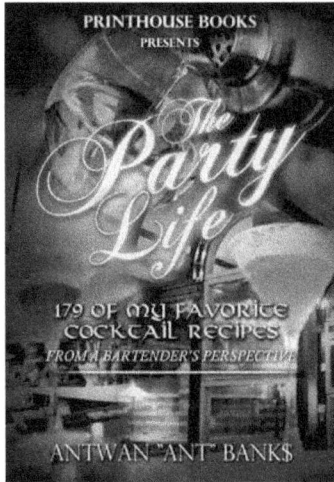

These collection of spirits; were some of my favorites to mix for the thousands of customers that I served as a bartender back in my 20's. During 1995 - 1996, I worked as a bartender in several Las Vegas Clubs and had a damn good time doing it! I've included a few recipes I picked up from fellow bartenders, some from customers and most I've learned from Bartending School.

ANTWAN BANK$

Mixology is an art and if mastered one can make a really good living serving spirits and conversing with the people you serve at your bar. If you're a bartender looking for some new drinks or you're just someone interested in mixing up some new drinks in your kitchen. This book of spirits is for you. Welcome to the Party Life and remember to drink responsibly.

Tahiry

Everlasting Romance, An American Love Story

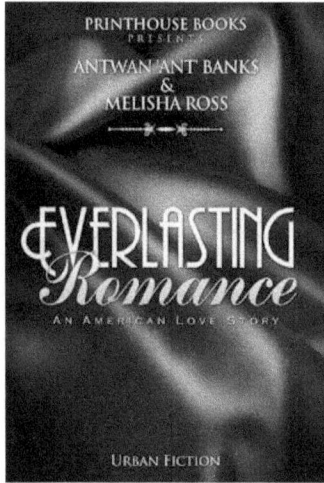

PRINTHOUSE BOOKS
PRESENTS

ANTWAN 'ANT' BANKS
&
MELISHA ROSS

EVERLASTING
Romance
AN AMERICAN LOVE STORY

URBAN FICTION

From the backdrop of the ATL; the hottest city in the South, comes a compelling love story about several friends and their adventures in College at the A.U and their professional careers while in the city of Atlanta. Experience Love, Drama, infidelity and historic memories as you indulge yourself in this Romantic tale of fiction. Set in 2001-2002, you're sure to reminisce back when Jay-Z, Nelly, Luda, Missy, 112, Lil Jon, Alicia Keys and more were in heavy rotation on your favorite radio station. When T.I's album;

I'm Serious had the city crazy, the clubs closed late and Ying Yang had those ATL Shake stages rocking and dollars raining.

Everlasting Romance, An American Love Story explores the essence of friendships, life, Love and how those bonds molded several individuals into a close knit family while in the hot city of Atlanta. Donnie, Quentin, Chantel, Cynthia and their friends; found themselves sharing love at every level; Brotherly, Sisterly and most of all intimately! But; at what cost!

Tahiry

www.PrintHouseBooks.com

Read it, Enjoy it, Tell a friend!

Atlanta, GA.

All titles available everywhere; that books are sold in the US, Canada, UK, Europe, Australia and New Zealand in Paperback, Hardcover and eBook.

VIP INK Publishing Group, Inc.

PRINTHOUSE BOOKS

Atlanta, GA.